KITCHEN
TABLE

100 Family Meals

ANNABEL KARMEL

www.mykitchentable.co.uk

Welcome to *my* KITCHEN TABLE

I have collected **100 of my favourite family meals** for you and your loved ones to enjoy. Nutritious, tasty and easy to prepare, they're guaranteed to please the whole family. I hope you share many happy meals together.

Annabel Karmel

www.annabelkarmel.com

KITCHEN
TABLE

0.0 Family Meals

KITCHEN TABLE gives you a wealth of recipes from your favourite chefs. Whether you want a quick weekday supper, sumptuous weekend feast or food for friends and family, let Rick, Ken, Madhur, Antonio, Ainsley, Mary and Annabel bring their expertise to your table.

For exclusive recipes, our regular newsletter, blog and news about Apps for your phone, visit www.mykitchentable.co.uk

Throughout this book, when you see visit our site for practical videos, tips and hints from the My Kitchen Table team.

Contents

Breakfast bites   6

Chicken   26

Fish   60

Meat   90

Veggie   114

Snacks   136

Sweet treats   170

Index   206

Annabel's granola

This delicious granola is very versatile. You can have it for breakfast with milk. It's also very good on its own as a snack or layered with yoghurt, honey and fruit. If your child is anti-nuts or allergic then you could substitute pumpkin seeds instead, or double the quantity of raisins.

Step one Preheat the oven to 150°C/300°F/gas 2.

Step two Put the oats, pecans, coconut, salt and sugar in a large bowl and mix with a wooden spoon.

Step three Whisk the oil and maple syrup together in a jug or small bowl. Pour over the oats and mix well.

Step four Spread out on a lightly oiled baking sheet and bake in the centre of the oven for 40–45 minutes, stirring every 10 minutes. Transfer to a bowl, stir in the raisins and leave to cool.

Wholegrain cereals are a good source of iron. However, it is difficult for our bodies to absorb iron from a non-meat source (red meat provides the most easily absorbed form of iron). To improve the absorption of iron from breakfast cereal you need to give your child vitamin C-rich fruit, such as kiwi or berry fruits, or vitamin C-rich juice, such as orange or cranberry juice.

Serves 6–8

175g (6oz) rolled oats

70g (2½ oz) coarsely chopped pecans

20g (¾oz) shredded/ desiccated coconut

¼ tsp salt

60g (2¼ oz) soft brown sugar

2 tbsp canola or sunflower oil

4 tbsp maple syrup

50g (2oz) raisins

French toast with caramelised apples

Challah, a plaited Jewish yeast bread made with eggs and butter, is traditionally served on Friday night in Jewish households, and is good for making French toast. Use slightly stale challah; brioche is a good alternative if you can't find any.

Serves 2

Caramelised apples

20g (¾oz) unsalted butter

2 tbsp caster sugar

2 medium apples, peeled, cored and cut into 12 wedges

French toast

2 thick slices slightly stale white bread, crusts removed

2 eggs

2 tbsp milk

1 tbsp caster sugar

3–4 drops vanilla essence

knob of butter, for frying

pinch of ground cinnamon, for sprinkling

Step one To make the caramelised apples, melt the butter in a frying pan over a medium heat. Stir in the sugar until dissolved. Add the apple slices and, turning them occasionally, cook for 5–10 minutes or until soft and just turning golden.

Step two For the French toast, cut the bread into fun shapes like animals or hearts (using cookie cutters), fingers or triangles. Beat the eggs with the milk, half a tablespoon of the caster sugar and the vanilla essence and pour into a shallow dish. Heat a frying pan over medium heat and add the knob of butter. Dip the bread into the beaten egg, making sure that it is thoroughly soaked, then fry each piece for 2–3 minutes or until golden on one side, then flip over and cook for another 2–3 minutes.

Step three Mix the remaining sugar and the cinnamon together and sprinkle over the hot French toast. Serve the caramelised apples on the side, or between layers of toast.

Instead of caramelised apples, try blueberry compote: put 100g blueberries in a pan, add 1 tablespoon of caster sugar and a squeeze of lemon juice. Heat gently until the blueberries pop open and release their juices, and then simmer for around 2–3 minutes.

Best ever banana bread

This banana bread is wonderfully moist and is great for breakfast or lunchboxes. This keeps well but you can also wrap slices in plastic wrap and freeze in plastic freezer bags. Many children aren't keen on nuts, so you can omit them from this recipe. Nut allergies are also a very real problem.

Cuts into 8 slices

Step one Preheat the oven to 180°C/350°F/gas 4. Grease and line a 22 x 11 x 7cm (8½ x 4½ x 2¾in) loaf tin.

Step two Beat the butter and sugar together until creamy then add the egg and continue to beat until smooth. Add the mashed bananas, yoghurt and vanilla essence.

Step three Sift together the flour, bicarbonate of soda, cinnamon and salt and beat this gradually into the banana mixture. Finally, stir in the raisins and chopped nuts (if using)

Step four Bake for about 1 hour or until a cocktail stick inserted in the centre comes out clean.

100g (4oz) butter

100g (4oz) brown sugar

1 egg

450g (1lb) bananas, mashed

45ml (3 tbsp) natural yoghurt

5ml (1 tsp) vanilla essence

225g (8oz) plain flour

1 tsp bicarbonate of soda

1 tsp ground cinnamon

½ teaspoon salt

100g (4oz) raisins

40g (1½ oz) chopped pecans or walnuts (optional)

rabbits

Welsh rarebit is a slightly enriched version of cheese on toast – children will probably enjoy this version of 'rabbit'. It is not suitable for freezing or reheating.

Serves 1

45g (1½ oz) Cheddar, grated

1 egg yolk

1 tsp cream or milk

2–3 drops Worcestershire sauce (or to taste)

pepper, to taste

1 muffin

Garnish

peas or mangetout

thin slices of carrot

1 black olive, stoned and halved

few fresh chives

Step one Preheat the grill to high.

Step two Put the cheese, egg, cream or milk and Worcestershire sauce into a bowl and mash together. Season to taste with pepper.

Step three Spread the cheese mixture over the cut sides of the toasted muffins, spreading right to the edges.

Step four Cook the two pieces under the grill around 7–8cm (about 3in) away from the heat source (one rack down from normal grilling position) – don't have them too close as the egg in the mixture can make them brown very quickly.

Step five Decorate the cooked muffins with peas for eyes and strips of carrot, mangetout or snow peas for ears, half an olive for a nose and chives for whiskers. Serve immediately.

Apple and carrot muffins w

This is one of my favourite muffin recipes, and they ᴄ
They are great for breakfast, lunchboxes or just a snacᴋ
flour helps to boost the fibre content and adding grated c
keeps the muffins moist and gives them a delicious fruit flav

Step one Preheat the oven to 180°C/350°F/gas 4 and line a muffin tray with paper cups.

Step two Combine the flour, sugar, skimmed milk powder, baking powder, cinnamon, ginger and salt in a mixing bowl.

Step three In a separate bowl, combine the oil, honey, maple syrup, eggs and vanilla essence. Beat lightly with a balloon whisk until blended. Add the grated apple, carrots and raisins to the liquid mixture and stir until just combined.

Step four Fill the cups until two-thirds full and bake for 20–25 minutes.

You can also make mini muffins – which are ideal for children – and they take about 15 minutes to bake.

Makes 12 larᵍ

150g (5oz) plain wholemeal flour

50g (2oz) granulated sugar

25g (1oz) dried skimmed milk powder

1½ tsp baking powder

½ tsp cinnamon

½ tsp ground ginger

¼ tsp salt

125ml (4½ fl oz) vegetable oil

50ml (2fl oz) honey

50ml (2fl oz) maple syrup

2 eggs, lightly beaten

½ tsp vanilla essence

1 large apple, peeled and grated

75g (3oz) carrots, peeled and grated

75g (3oz) raisins

**⌐p of
…lsa)**

…pe tomato,
…d deseeded

…g onion, thinly
…d

… red chilli, deseeded
or to taste

1 tsp lemon juice

Burrito filling

1 small (60g/2¼ oz)
red onion, thinly sliced

½ (60g/2¼ oz) red
pepper, deseeded and
thinly sliced

1 tbsp sunflower or
olive oil

1 tsp balsamic vinegar

large pinch of smoked
spanish paprika or
pinch of coriander

Scrambled eggs

30g (1oz) butter

3 eggs

1 tbsp chopped
coriander (optional)

2 large soft tortilla
wraps

sour cream (optional),
to serve

Step one Mix the salsa ingredients together and season with salt and pepper. Set aside.

Step two For the filling, sauté the onion and pepper in the oil for 8–10 minutes or until soft. Add the balsamic vinegar and smoked paprika or coriander and cook for 1 minute. Set aside to cool slightly while you scramble the eggs.

Step three Melt the butter in a saucepan and add the eggs. Cook, stirring until softly scrambled, stir in the coriander (if using) and season to taste with salt and pepper. Warm the tortillas in a microwave for about 10 seconds or in a dry frying pan for about 30 seconds.

Step four Divide the onion and pepper mixture between the tortillas, keeping it in the centre. Add the eggs, then a spoonful of salsa. Fold the edges in then roll up the tortilla to make a burrito. If you like you can serve with a little sour cream.

The salsa and sweet pepper and onion mixture can be made ahead. Cover and refrigerate until needed. Warm the pepper mixture in a saucepan or in the microwave (15–20 seconds).

To skin tomatoes: cut a cross in the base of each tomato, put in a bowl and cover with boiling water from a freshly boiled kettle. Leave for about 30 seconds. Drain the tomatoes and put in a bowl of cold water. When the tomatoes are cool enough to handle, peel off the skin.

Annabel's favourite panca.

It's fun to make pancakes, particularly when you tr)
catching them in the pan. I love these thin pancakes w
filling and irresistible warm toffee sauce. They are also ɡ
plain with lemon and sugar or with a little golden syrup.

Step one Measure the caster sugar and flour into a bowl. Make a well in the centre. Crack in the eggs, then slowly add the milk and beat until smooth.

Step two Heat the oil in a small omelette pan. Pour a little of the mixture into the pan and tilt to coat the pan and cook for 2–3 minutes. Carefully turn over and cook on the other side, then slide onto a plate while you make the rest.

Step three Place one pancake on a board and then spread a tablespoon of cream cheese in the centre. Arrange a few slices of strawberries over the cream cheese. Fold in half and then in half again. Repeat with the remaining pancakes.

Step four To make the toffee sauce, melt the butter in a small pan. Add the sugar and cream and slowly bring to the boil. Remove from the heat and add the vanilla. Pour a little of the sauce over the pancakes to serve.

Makes 8 par.
150g (5oz) plair.
15g (½ oz) caster sugar
2 eggs
250ml (8fl oz) milk
2 tbsp sunflower oil
125g (5oz) light cream cheese
200g (7oz) strawberries, sliced

Toffee sauce
50g (2oz) butter
50g (2oz) light brown sugar
150 ml (¼ pint) double cream
½ tsp vanilla essence

oars with cranberries,
.npkin seeds

oack-type bars are packed full of nutritious

s

ε) butter

⁄oz) brown
ar

0g (2¼ oz) golden
syrup

½ tsp salt

130g (4½ oz) porridge
oats

35g (1¼ oz) dried
apple, chopped

35g (1¼ oz) dried
apricots, chopped

25g (1oz) dried
cranberries

25g (1oz) pumpkin
seeds

2 tbsp sunflower seeds

25g (1oz) desiccated
coconut

Step one Preheat the oven to 180°C/350°F/gas 4. Line and grease the tin.

Step two In a saucepan, melt together the butter, sugar, golden syrup and salt.

Step three Mix all the dry ingredients together in a bowl and stir in the butter and syrup mixture. Spoon the mixture into a 20cm (8in) square baking tin and press down with a potato masher to level the surface.

Step four Bake in the oven for 18–20 minutes. Store in the fridge and cut into bars before serving.

Jamaican banana muffins

The smell of these baking should lure many children into the kitche eager for the crisp cinnamon crust and moist banana muffin underne For maximum flavour, make sure that you use very ripe bananas.

Step one Preheat the oven to 180°C/350°F/gas 4 and line a muffin tin with 8 paper cases.

Step two Mix together the sunflower oil and sugar. Add the mashed bananas and mix thoroughly. Finally, beat the egg with a fork, add to the banana mixture and mix again.

Step three Sift the flours, salt, bicarbonate of soda and ground cinnamon into a medium-sized bowl. Tip in the little bits that were sieved out of the wholemeal flour. Add half the flour mixture to the banana mixture and mix well. Add the hot water and mix in thoroughly. Mix in the remaining flour and the raisins. Divide the mixture between the paper cases.

Step four Bake for 25–30 minutes or until the muffins are well risen and spring back gently when you press the tops. Transfer to a wire rack to cool. If you like, you can sprinkle the tops of the muffins with brown sugar.

For a gluten-free version: use 60g (2¼oz) sunflower oil, 160g (5⅓oz) gluten-free flour, 1 teaspoon bicarbonate of soda and 2 tablespoons hot milk instead of water. Bake for 30–35 minutes.

Makes 8 muffins

75ml (2½ fl oz) sunflower oil

100g (4oz) light muscovado sugar

250g (9oz) very ripe bananas (unpeeled weight), mashed

1 medium egg

140g (5oz) plain flour

20g (¾oz) wholemeal flour

½ tsp salt

½ tsp bicarbonate of soda

¼ tbsp ground cinnamon

3 tbsp very hot water

75g (2½oz) raisins

3 tsp brown sugar (optional)

Have you made this recipe? Tell us what you think at www.mykitchentable.co.uk/blog

and banana smoothie

icy peaches
ll banana
sp vanilla yoghurt
tsp honey
2 tbsp milk

Step one Put the peaches in a small bowl, pour over boiling water and leave for about 30 seconds. Remove and run the peaches under the cold tap. The skins should then peel off easily. Cut the flesh into chunks.

Step two Blend the peaches together with the banana, yoghurt, honey and milk.

Watermelon cocktail

Serves 2

300g (10½ oz)
watermelon flesh, cut
into chunks

100ml (3fl oz) freshly
squeezed orange juice

2 tbsp icing sugar

Step one Simply blend together the melon, orange juice and icing sugar.

Cherry and berry crush

Serves 2

125g (4½ oz) cherries

60g (2¼ oz) each
strawberries and
raspberries

50ml (2fl oz) raspberry
drinking yoghurt

4 tsp icing sugar (to
taste)

Step one Stone the cherries and blend all the ingredients together.

Annabel's pad Thai

This tasty pad Thai is very popular. You could make this a vegetaria...
version by replacing the chicken with more vegetables. It is not suitab...
for freezing.

Step one Cut the chicken into strips, then mix together the ingredients for the marinade and marinate the chicken for 30 minutes.

Step two Cook the noodles according to the instructions on the packet. Lightly beat the eggs with a little salt, then cook in a frying pan (approx. 20 cm diameter) in ½ tbsp of the sunflower oil to make a thin omelette. Next, roll up the omelette and cut it into strips, then set aside.

Step three Heat 1 tablespoon of the oil in a wok or large frying pan. Stir-fry the shallots or onion for about 3–4 minutes. Sprinkle with a generous pinch of caster sugar and stir-fry for 1 minute, then add the garlic and chilli (if using) and cook for 1 more minute. Add the chicken strips and stir-fry for 3–4 minutes until cooked. Remove from the wok and set aside.

Step four Heat the remaining 1½ tablespoons of oil in the wok. Add the leek and stir-fry for 3 minutes. Cut the broccoli into small florets then add it and the beansprouts to the wok (reserving a couple of handfuls of beansprouts) and stir-fry for 4 minutes. Add the chicken, cooked drained noodles and strips of egg with the vinegar, soy, fish and sweet chilli sauces. Cook until the noodles are warmed through.

Step five Serve in bowls with the reserved raw beansprouts sprinkled over.

Serves 6

Marinade

1 tbsp each soy sauce and sake

1½ tsp sugar

1½ tsp cornstarch

250g (9oz) chicken breast

150g (5oz) medium rice noodles

2 eggs

3 tbsp sunflower oil, for frying

2 shallots, finely sliced, or 1 onion

¼ tsp caster sugar

1 garlic clove, crushed

½ red chilli, finely sliced (optional)

1 leek, thinly sliced

100g (3½ oz) broccoli

200g (7oz) beansprouts

2 tbsp rice wine vinegar

2 tbsp soy sauce

3 tsp fish sauce

2 tbsp sweet chilli sauce

∴n satay with chinese leaf cabbage,
∴prouts and baby sweetcorn

ıs a very tasty way to get a healthy dose of protein.

∴erves 2

Marinade

1 tbsp smooth peanut
butter

1½ tbsp soy sauce

1½ tbsp honey

1 tbsp sunflower oil

freshly ground black
pepper

1 breast of chicken
(approx. 125g/4½ oz),
cut into cubes

50g (2oz) baby corn,
cut into strips

Dressing

2 tbsp sesame oil

2 tbsp sunflower oil

1 tbsp soy sauce

1 tbsp rice wine
vinegar

1 tsp fresh grated
ginger

2 tsp honey

85g (3oz) beansprouts

85g (3oz) chinese leaf
cabbage, shredded

Step one Mix together the ingredients for the marinade and marinate the chicken for about 30 minutes. Soak four bamboo skewers in water and preheat the grill to high.

Step two Thread the chicken onto the skewers and arrange on a baking sheet lined with aluminium foil. Grill for about 5 minutes on each side.

Step three Steam the baby corn for 4 minutes and leave to cool.

Step four Mix together the ingredients for the dressing. In a bowl, mix together the baby corn, beansprouts and chinese leaf cabbage and toss with the dressing. Stick the chicken skewers into the salad. This is best served when the chicken is still warm.

Caroline's lasagne alfredo

Lasagne tends to be popular with children, so it's a good idea to combine the pasta itself with some other nutritious ingredients. This delicious lasagne is made with chicken and spinach. You can use fresh lasagne or the dried, no precook variety – but I prefer fresh. This dish is suitable for freezing.

Step one Preheat the oven to 200°C/400°F/gas 6.

Step two Melt the butter in a medium pan and sauté the onion for 5–6 minutes until softening and just starting to turn golden. Add the garlic and cook for 1 minute, then stir in the flour and cook for 1 minute.

Step three Remove from the heat and gradually stir in the stock and milk. Cook over a medium heat, stirring constantly until the sauce thickens and comes to a simmer. Remove from the heat, cool for a minute, then stir in the Cheddar and Parmesan and season well with salt, pepper and nutmeg.

Step four Cook the spinach in a large pan until wilted. Cool, then squeeze out as much liquid as possible and chop roughly.

Step five Put a thin layer of sauce in the bottom of a 24 x 15cm (8 x 5in) ovenproof dish and add a layer of lasagne sheets. Scatter over half of the spinach and chicken, season with salt and pepper and spoon over one-third of the sauce. Add a further layer of lasagne, and repeat layers of spinach, chicken, seasoning, sauce and lasagne. Top with the remaining sauce and sprinkle over the reserved Parmesan. Bake for 40–45 minutes until piping hot in the centre. Allow to stand for around 15 minutes before serving.

Serves 6

250g (9oz) spinach, washed

9 sheets dried, no-precook lasagne

2 chicken breasts, about 110g (4oz) each, thinly sliced

Sauce

60g (2oz) butter

1 small onion, finely chopped

1 garlic clove, crushed

60g (2¼ oz) plain flour

350ml (12fl oz) chicken stock

300ml (10fl oz) milk

110g (4oz) Cheddar, grated

50g (2¼ oz) freshly grated Parmesan (reserve 4 tbsp for the topping)

salt, freshly ground black pepper and grated nutmeg, to season

Maple-glazed griddled chicken

This slightly sweet combination of ketchup, maple syrup and smoked paprika should tempt fussy eaters. The paprika gives the chicken a rich flavour and orange hue. Sweet smoked paprika is available in some supermarkets, Spanish delicatessens and also online from delicioso.co.uk. Be careful not to use hot paprika by mistake!

Serves 4

4 skinned chicken breasts

light olive oil, for griddling

Marinade

5 tbsp vegetable oil

5 tbsp tomato ketchup

3 tbsp maple syrup

3 tsp sweet smoked paprika

Step one First, flatten the chicken. One good way to do so is to slit one side of a plastic freezer bag so that you can position the meat inside then cover with the plastic. Use a heavy smooth-sided mallet to pound the chicken, working from the middle outwards to a uniform thickness. Alternatively, cover with cling film and bash a few times with a mallet.

Step two For the marinade, whisk together the vegetable oil, ketchup, maple syrup and paprika, pour over the chicken and leave to marinate for a couple of hours.

Step three Heat a griddle, brush with a little olive oil and griddle the chicken for about 4 minutes on each side or until cooked through, basting occasionally. Pour over any extra juices to serve.

I like to cook marinated chicken on the griddle. A griddle is a healthy way of cooking as it uses little fat and keeps the chicken tender and moist. You can also griddle vegetables such as sliced courgettes and sweet peppers. You can use an ordinary griddle, but one of the best pieces of kitchen equipment that I have is a contact griddle and grill. It works for everything from chicken and hamburgers to fish and vegetables. It griddles both sides of the chicken at once, cutting the cooking time in half.

my
KITCHEN
TABLE

Have you made this recipe? Tell us what you think at
www.mykitchentable.co.uk /blog

32

Chicken Karmel

This sweet and sour chicken recipe is a great favourite with children and my family loves it. Serve with fluffy white rice. If your child isn't keen on green beans or baby sweetcorn, use different vegetables.

Step one For the batter, in a small bowl, beat together the egg yolk, cornflour and milk.

Step two Mix together all the ingredients for the sweet and sour sauce.

Step three Heat 2 tablespoons of the oil in a wok, dip the chicken into the batter, then fry for 3–4 minutes until golden. Remove from the wok and set aside.

Step four Heat the remaining vegetable oil in a wok and stir-fry the carrot, baby corn and green beans for 2 minutes. Add the sauce, bring to the boil and cook for 2 minutes. Remove from the heat and stir in the spring onions. Add the chicken to the vegetables and heat through. Season to taste.

To make eating fun you can buy child-friendly plastic chopsticks that are joined at the top so that they only need to be squeezed together to pick up food. This recipe would be perfect for these as everything is cut into bite-sized pieces.

Serves 4

Batter

1 egg yolk

1½ tbsp cornflour

1 tbsp milk

Sweet and sour sauce

1 tbsp soy sauce

2 tbsp tomato ketchup

2 tbsp rice wine vinegar

2 tbsp caster sugar

¼ tsp sesame oil

4 tbsp vegetable oil

250g (9oz) chicken breasts, cut into bite-sized cubes

75g (3oz) carrot, cut into matchsticks

50g (2oz) baby corn, sliced in half lengthways, then in half across

50g (2oz) fine green beans, topped and tailed and cut in half

2 spring onions, finely sliced

salt and freshly ground black pepper

Delicious chicken fajitas

To save time, you could use a bought tomato salsa for this easy dish.

Makes 6 fajitas

2 small chicken breasts

⅛ tsp paprika

⅛ tsp mild chilli powder

⅛ tsp cumin (optional)

¼ tsp oregano

1 tbsp plus 1 tsp olive oil

1 garlic clove, crushed

1 onion, peeled and thinly sliced

½ small red pepper (capsicum), deseeded and thinly sliced

Tomato salsa

¼ green pepper

½ onion

½ red or green chilli

½ tbsp olive oil

1 small garlic clove, chopped

½ tsp red wine vinegar

1 x 200g (7oz) tin chopped tomatoes

salt and freshly ground black pepper

½ tbsp parsley, chopped

8 small flour tortillas

75g (3oz) shredded iceberg lettuce

75g (3oz) Cheddar, grated

3 tbsp sour cream

Step one Cut the chicken into strips, and toss it in the paprika, chilli powder, cumin and oregano. Heat 1 tsp of the oil in a pan and sauté the chicken, stirring occasionally, for 3–4 minutes. Remove the chicken with a slotted spoon.

Step two Add the remaining tablespoon of oil and sauté the garlic, onion and red pepper for 5 minutes. Return the chicken to the pan, season to taste and heat through.

Step three To make the salsa, deseed and dice the green pepper, then peel and chop the onion and finely slice the chilli. Heat the oil and fry the chilli, onion, pepper and garlic for about 5 minutes. Add the vinegar and cook for about 20 seconds. Add the chopped tomatoes, salt and pepper and parsley and simmer, uncovered, for about 15 minutes.

Step three To assemble, heat the tortillas in the microwave or frying pan according to the packet instructions. Then place some of the chicken mixture along the centre of each tortilla, top with some tomato salsa, shredded lettuce, grated cheese and a little sour cream and roll up.

My favourite chicken fingers

Marinating chicken in buttermilk gives it a delicious flavour and tenderises the chicken. You are much better off making your own 'healthy fast food' as you are in control of the ingredients and there are no artificial colours or flavourings.

Step one Cut each chicken breast into 2-cm (½-in) strips and season with salt and freshly ground pepper.

Step two Combine the buttermilk, lemon juice, Worcestershire sauce, soy sauce, paprika and garlic in a bowl. Add the chicken strips and toss to coat. Cover and marinate for at least 1 hour or overnight.

Step three Drain the chicken well. In a large bowl, toss the breadcrumbs with the sesame seeds and some salt and pepper. Heat the oil in a large frying pan. Roll the chicken in the crumbs to coat and sauté until golden and cooked through, turning occasionally.

Serves 4

2 chicken breasts

200ml (7fl oz) buttermilk

1 tbsp lemon juice

1 tsp Worcestershire sauce

1 tsp soy sauce

¼ tsp paprika

1 garlic clove, peeled and sliced

136g (4½ oz) dried breadcrumbs or fresh white breadcrumbs

40g (1½ oz) sesame seeds

little vegetable oil for frying

salt and freshly ground black pepper

Chicken cannelloni

There are so may things that you can stuff inside cannelloni tubes, such as spinach and ricotta or Bolognese, but here's something a little different – tasty minced chicken with tomatoes covered with a creamy cheese sauce and a golden topping.

Serves 4

1 tbsp olive oil

1 onion, peeled and chopped

1 small garlic clove, crushed

40g (1½ oz) mushrooms, chopped

½ tsp dried mixed herbs

225g (8oz) minced chicken

1 x 200g (7 oz) can tomatoes or ½ x 400g (14oz) can

½ tbsp tomato ketchup

Cheese sauce

30g (1¼ oz) butter

30g (1¼ oz) flour

½ tsp paprika

400ml (14fl oz) milk

100g (3½ oz) Cheddar, grated

8 no pre-cook cannelloni tubes

Step one Heat the oil in a saucepan and sauté the onion and garlic for 2 minutes. Add the mushrooms, herbs and chicken and sauté for 3 minutes. Stir in the chopped tomatoes and ketchup and simmer for 20 minutes.

Step two Preheat the oven to 180°C/350°F/Gas 4, then make the cheese sauce. Melt the butter, then stir in the flour and paprika and cook for 1 minute. Gradually whisk in the milk. Bring to the boil and then simmer, stirring, until thickened. Stir in 50g (2oz) of the grated Cheddar.

Step three Stuff the cannelloni tubes with the chicken filling and arrange them in a shallow ovenproof dish. Pour over the cheese sauce, sprinkle with the remaining Cheddar cheese and bake in the oven for 25 minutes.

Basket-weave chicken breasts

The bright orange and green basket-weave pattern made by ... and courgette strips looks sensational wrapped around these stuffed chicken breasts. If your child prefers, you can stuff the chicken breasts with cheese and ham.

Step one Using a potato peeler, cut the carrot and courgette lengthways into long thin strips. Blanch them in boiling water for just under 1 minute and place on absorbent kitchen paper to dry.

Step two To prepare the mushroom stuffing, sauté the shallot in the butter and oil until softened, add the chopped mushrooms and cook for 3–4 minutes. Add the parsley, lemon juice and breadcrumbs and cook for 2 minutes. Season to taste.

Step three Cut a slit in each of the chicken breasts to form a pocket and stuff with the mushroom mixture. Season the chicken.

Step four Place five strips of courgette horizontally quite close together on top of a piece of plastic food wrap (suitable for cooking) just big enough to wrap around the chicken breast. Weave five strips of carrot vertically through the courgette strips to make a basket-weave pattern. Wrap the plastic food wrap and woven vegetables around the chicken breasts to form a parcel. Cook in a steamer for about 20 minutes or until cooked through.

Step five To make the sauce, put the stock and lime or lemon juice into a small saucepan and bring to the boil. Remove from the heat and whisk in the butter. Stir in the tarragon and cream and season to taste. To serve, pour some of the sauce on to a plate, remove the plastic food wrap and place the chicken breasts on top of the sauce.

Serves 2

1 large carrot

1 large courgette

1 shallot, finely chopped

75g (3oz) button mushrooms, chopped

knob of butter

½ tbsp vegetable oil

1 tsp fresh chopped parsley

a squeeze of fresh lemon juice

1 tbsp breadcrumbs

salt and freshly ground black pepper

2 large chicken breasts

Tarragon sauce

60ml (2¼ fl oz) chicken stock

1½ tbsp fresh lime or lemon juice

50g (2oz) cold butter, cut into cubes

½ tbsp chopped tarragon

2 tbsp double cream

ıcken yakitori with noodles

Chicken doesn't always have to be covered in breadcrumbs. One of my favourite ways of preparing chicken is to make these marinated yakitori chicken skewers. Mirin is a sweetened sake or rice wine with a light syrupy texture and it adds a wonderful taste to these skewers.

Serves 3

3 tbsp mirin

3 tbsp honey

3 tbsp soy sauce

2 tsp rice wine vinegar

1 tsp grated fresh ginger

1 garlic clove, crushed

3 tbsp oil

4 chicken thighs, boned and cut into large chunks

125g (4¼ oz) medium noodles

1 large courgette, sliced into batons

1 large carrot, sliced into batons

2 spring onions, thinly sliced

1 red onion, sliced

75g (3oz) chestnut mushrooms, sliced

75ml (3fl oz) chicken stock

4 tsp soy sauce

4 tsp sweet chilli sauce

Step one Preheat the oven to 220°C/425°F/gas 7.

Step two Measure the mirin, soy sauce, honey, vinegar, ginger and garlic into a small pan. Bring to the boil then reduce by a third, stirring.

Step three Mix the cold marinade with the chicken and marinate for 30 minutes. Season and thread onto 6 skewers. Heat 2 tbsp of the oil in a frying pan. Brown the skewers for 2-3 minutes on both sides until golden, then place on a baking sheet. Bake in the oven for 10-12 minutes until cooked through.

Step four Meanwhile, cook the noodles in boiling salted water according to the packet instructions and drain.

Step five Heat the remaining oil in a frying pan or wok. Fry all of the vegetables for about 4 minutes, then add the noodles and stock, water, chilli sauce, soy and seasoning and heat through. Serve with the kebabs.

Turkey meatballs with spaghetti and tomato sauce

Turkey is often used as a low-fat substitute to chicken. It is sometimes accused of not being as tasty, but these meatballs are absolutely delicious.

Step one Heat the oil in a pan and fry the onions gently for about 10 minutes.

Step two Meanwhile, soak the breadcrumbs in milk for 10 minutes in a large bowl.

Step three To make the sauce, transfer half the sautéed onion to a pan, add all the other sauce ingredients and simmer for 10 minutes.

Step four To make the meatballs, add the turkey mince, thyme, the remaining sautéed onion, salt and black pepper to the soaked breadcrumbs and mix together. Using floured hands, form teaspoons of the turkey mixture into small balls. Heat the sunflower oil in a frying pan and brown the meatballs. Transfer the meatballs to the pan of tomato sauce and simmer, uncovered, for 10 minutes.

Step five Cook the spaghetti according to the instructions on the packet. Drain and toss with the sauce.

Serves 4

Turkey meatballs

2 tbsp olive oil

2 medium onions (approx.175g/6oz), chopped

40g (1½ oz) white breadcrumbs (approx. 2 slices)

50ml (2fl oz) milk

250g (9oz) turkey mince

1 tsp fresh thyme

½ tsp salt and freshly ground black pepper

1 tbsp flour, to dust hands

2 tbsp sunflower oil, for frying

Tomato sauce

½ the chopped onions from above

1 x 400g (14oz) tin chopped tomatoes

100ml (3½ fl oz) water

1 tbsp tomato purée

2 tsp sugar

¼ tsp oregano

pinch of dried chilli flakes

salt and freshly ground black pepper

250g (9oz) spaghetti

Japanese chicken salad

A delicious chicken salad made with Thai jasmine rice. You can buy this in most supermarkets – it's quite similar to sushi rice. The crunchy texture of the cucumber and red pepper contrasts well with the rice and the dressing gives the salad a delicious flavour that is not too strong, so should attract fussy eaters. This would make a good addition to your child's lunchbox.

Serves 2–3

110g (4oz) Thai jasmine rice

⅓ cucumber

3 spring onions, sliced

½ red pepper, diced

85g (3oz) cooked chicken, diced

¼ avocado, diced (optional)

salt and pepper, to taste

Dressing

2 tbsp rice wine vinegar

1 tbsp caster sugar

½ tbsp sunflower oil

Step one Put the rice in a large pan with plenty of cold water and a pinch of salt. Bring to the boil and simmer for 12–15 minutes until the rice is just tender. Drain and leave to stand in a sieve for 15 minutes, stirring halfway through, then transfer to a bowl.

Step two To make the dressing, gently warm the rice wine vinegar and sugar until the sugar has dissolved. Add the sunflower oil and stir into the rice. Leave until cold and refrigerate (if using for a lunchbox).

Step three Cut the cucumber in half lengthways and scoop out the seeds with a teaspoon. Dice the flesh. Stir into the dressed rice with the spring onions, pepper, chicken and avocado (if using) and season to taste.

Nasi goreng

This is a delicious Indonesian rice dish. Traditionally it also contains some chopped roasted peanuts and you can add some if you like and you could also add some chopped red chilli with the garlic.

Step one Cook the rice in boiling water according to the packet instructions and drain.

Step two Mix the chicken with the soy, sesame oil and sugar – leave to marinate for 30 minutes.

Step three Heat the oil in a large frying pan. Add the onions and red pepper and gently fry for 5 minutes. Add the garlic, then the chicken. Fry for 4 minutes. Add the corn, curry paste and peas and fry for another 4–5 minutes. Add the rice and toss together. Season to taste and add the spring onions to garnish.

Serves 4

250g (9oz) rice

2 chicken breasts, diced

3 tbsp soy sauce

½ tbsp sesame oil

1 tbsp brown sugar

2 tbsp vegetable oil

2 large onions, finely chopped

1 red pepper, diced

1 garlic clove, crushed

90g (3½ oz) baby corn, sliced

1–2 tsp mild korma curry paste

90g (3oz) frozen peas

3 spring onions, finely sliced, to garnish

Annabel's pasta salad with marinated chicken and roasted peppers

This is one of my favourite salads. Roasting peppers in the oven gives them a deliciously sweet flavour. You could marinate two uncooked chicken breasts for about 10 minutes in some olive oil, rice wine vinegar and pesto, then griddle the chicken and serve this as a warm salad. It is not suitable for freezing.

Serves 4

1 red pepper, sliced in half and deseeded

1 yellow pepper, sliced in half and deseeded

1 tsp Dijon mustard

4 tbsp olive oil

3 tbsp rice wine vinegar

1 tbsp green pesto

2 cooked chicken breasts, thinly sliced

2 tbsp parsley, chopped

2 spring onions, finely sliced

½ garlic clove, crushed

150g (5oz) fusilli, cooked and refreshed in cold water

50g (2oz) pea shoots or watercress

salt and freshly ground black pepper

Step one Preheat the oven to 200°C/400°F/gas 6.

Step two Place the red and yellow peppers, cut-side down, on a baking sheet. Roast in the oven for 20–25 minutes until soft and the skins are dark brown. Remove from the oven, place in a bowl, cover with cling film and leave to cool. Once cool enough to handle, remove the skins and slice the flesh into thin strips.

Step three Mix together the Dijon mustard, oil, rice wine vinegar and pesto in a large bowl. Add the chicken, parsley, spring onions, garlic and cooked pasta and toss together with the peppers. Leave to marinate in the fridge for 1 hour.

Step four Scatter a few of the pea shoots or watercress leaves on the base of a serving plate. Roughly chop the remaining leaves and fold into the salad with some salt and pepper. Spoon the salad onto the serving plate.

Fruity chicken curry

An all-time favourite with my family. Simple to make, but with a delicious mild, fruity curry flavour. It's great served with poppadoms and fluffy white rice. Suitable for freezing.

Step one Heat 1 tablespoon of the oil in a wok or frying pan and stir-fry the chicken for about 4 minutes. Remove the chicken and set aside.

Step two Heat the remaining oil in the wok and sauté the onion and garlic for 3 minutes, then add the apple and baby corn and stir-fry for 3 minutes.

Step three Add the korma curry paste, mango chutney, tomato purée, coconut milk, chicken stock and chicken pieces and simmer for about 12 minutes. Add the frozen peas and cook for 3 to 4 minutes. Season to taste.

Serves 2

3 tbsp vegetable oil

2 chicken breasts, cut into chunks

1 onion, peeled and chopped

1 garlic clove, crushed

1 medium apple, peeled and thinly sliced

100g (3½ oz) baby corn, cut into quarters

1 heaped tbsp korma curry paste

¼ tbsp mango chutney

1 tbsp tomato purée

150ml (¼ pint) coconut milk

1 chicken stock cube, dissolved in 150ml (¼ pint) boiling water

100g (3½ oz) frozen peas

salt and freshly ground black pepper

Thai-style chicken soup

Thai-style food tends to be very popular with children. This easy-to-prepare soup is ready in about 10 minutes and is almost a meal in itself. Suitable for freezing.

Serves 4

1 tbsp light olive oil

150g (5oz) chopped onion

1 garlic clove, crushed

½ red chilli, finely chopped (approx. 1 tbsp)

1 chicken breast fillet, cut into thin strips

100g (3½ oz) broccoli

600ml (1 pint) chicken stock

300ml (10fl oz) coconut milk

salt and freshly ground black pepper

150g (5oz) cooked rice (40g/1½ oz uncooked weight)

Step one Heat the oil in a pan and sauté the onion, garlic and chilli for 2 minutes. Add the strips of chicken and sauté for 2 more minutes.

Step two Cut the broccoli into small florets. Add the broccoli and chicken stock, bring to the boil and simmer for 4 minutes. Stir in the coconut milk and simmer for 2 minutes. Season to taste and stir in the cooked rice.

Singapore noodles

Children often have more adventurous tastes than we might imagine and I find that they enjoy oriental-style recipes like these noodles, particularly if you give them 'child-friendly' chopsticks that are joined at the top to eat them with. Not suitable for freezing.

Step one Mix together the ingredients for the marinade and marinate the chicken for about 30 minutes.

Step two Cook the noodles in boiling water according to the instructions on the packet. Drain.

Step three Heat the oil in a wok and stir-fry the carrots for 4 minutes. Add the garlic and chilli and stir-fry for 30 seconds. Add the chicken and stir-fry until just cooked. Stir in the korma curry paste, coconut milk, chicken stock and fish sauce. Then stir in the peas and sweetcorn and cook for about 3 minutes or until both the chicken and peas are cooked. About 2 minutes before the end of the cooking time, stir in the drained noodles

Serves 4

Marinade

2 tsp each soy sauce and salt

1 tsp sugar

1 tsp cornstarch

200g (7oz) chicken breast, cut into strips

100g (3½ oz) fine Chinese noodles

2 tbsp vegetable oil

150g (5¼ oz) carrots, cut into matchsticks

1 garlic clove, crushed

½ red chilli, deseeded and finely sliced

1 heaped tbsp korma curry paste (I used Patak's)

100ml (3½ fl oz) coconut milk

50ml (2fl oz) strong chicken stock (made with 2 tsp of chicken stock powder)

4 drops fish sauce

50g (2oz) frozen peas

50g (2oz) tinned sweetcorn

Salmon teriyaki

Oily fish like salmon, trout, tuna and mackerel contain omega-3 fatty acids, which protect against heart disease and strokes. The old wives' tale that fish is good for the brain is therefore true, as omega-3 essential fats optimize messaging between nerve cells in the brain. This is vital for proper brain functioning and research suggests that a diet rich in omega-3 fats can also improve the performance of children who suffer attention-deficit hyperactivity disorder or are dyspraxic.

Serves 4

Marinade

80ml (2¾fl oz) soy sauce

100ml (3½fl oz) sake

50ml (2fl oz) mirin (sweet sake for cooking)

2 tbsp sugar

4 x 150g (5¼oz) thick fillets of salmon, skinned

2 tbsp vegetable oil

150g (5¼oz) button mushrooms, sliced

150g (5¼oz) beansprouts

Step one Mix the ingredients for the marinade together in a saucepan and stir over a medium heat until the sugar has dissolved. Marinate the salmon in the sauce for 10 minutes.

Step two Heat half the oil and sauté the mushrooms for 2 minutes, then add the beansprouts and cook for 2 minutes more. Meanwhile, drain the salmon, reserving the marinade. Heat the remaining oil in a frying pan and sauté the salmon for 1 or 2 minutes on each side or until slightly browned. Pour away the excess oil from the frying pan. Alternatively, it is particularly good if you cook the salmon on a very hot griddle pan brushed with a little oil. Whichever method you choose, after 2 minutes pour a little of the teriyaki marinade over the salmon and continue to cook for a few minutes, basting occasionally. Simmer the remaining marinade in a small saucepan until thickened.

Step three Divide the vegetables between four plates, place the salmon on top and pour the teriyaki sauce over the fish.

For a video masterclass on filleting salmon, go to www.mykitchentable.co.uk/videos/filleting

Annabel's paella

You can add lots of different ingredients to paella. Although prawns and chicken are the main ingredients here, adding sausage can be good too (see tip below). Suitable for freezing.

Step one Heat the oil in a fairly large pan and sauté the onion and red pepper for 1 minute, then lower the heat and cook, covered, for about 10 minutes or until softened. Add the garlic and cook for 1 minute.

Step two Turn the heat up to high and sauté the chicken strips for 2–3 minutes or until the chicken turns white. Add the smoked paprika and the rice and cook gently for 2 minutes. Add the chopped tomatoes.

Step three Mix together the stock and tomato purée and pour this over the rice. Give it a quick stir and add the chilli flakes and salt. Cover and cook over a low heat for 12–15 minutes or until the rice is tender (check cooking instructions on the packet).

Step four Add the prawns and peas for the last 2 to 3 minutes. Finally, stir in the chopped spring onions.

Sausage is a nice addition, either slices of ordinary, cooked sausages or chorizo, which has a smoky taste. If you use chorizo, add about 50g (2oz) of it with the chicken and leave out the smoked paprika, using ordinary paprika instead.

Serves 4

1 tbsp vegetable oil

1 onion, finely chopped

75g (3oz) red pepper (approx. ½ pepper)

1 garlic clove, crushed or finely chopped

1 chicken breast (approx. 125g/4½ oz), cut into strips

½ tsp smoked paprika or ordinary paprika

200g (7oz) long grain rice

3 tomatoes (approx. 200g/7oz), deseeded and cut into 1 cm cubes

500ml (17¼ fl oz) chicken stock

1 tbsp tomato purée

pinch of dried chilli flakes

¼ tsp salt

75g (3oz) peeled prawns

110g (4oz) frozen peas

3 spring onions, finely sliced

Bag-baked cod niçoise

Here are the flavours of the south of France in individual parcels. Baking fish in a parcel keeps it wonderfully moist and seals in the flavour. You might think it strange that I am using olives – my daughter liked eating olives at the age of two and, surprisingly, they are popular with quite a few children. If your child doesn't like olives you could use four chopped sunblush tomatoes instead.

Serves 4

1 small red onion, diced

1 tsp olive oil

1 small garlic clove, crushed

1 tsp balsamic vinegar

½ tsp sugar

225g (8oz) cherry tomatoes, quartered

6–7 stoned black olives, quartered

4 skinless cod fillets, about 150g (5¼ oz) each

salt and pepper, to taste

12 basil leaves, to serve (optional)

Step one Preheat the oven to 200°C/400°F/gas 6.

Step two Sauté the onion in the oil for 7–8 minutes until soft. Add the garlic and balsamic vinegar and cook until the vinegar has evaporated, then stir in the sugar, tomatoes and olives and cook for 2–3 minutes, until the tomatoes start to soften. Remove from the heat and season to taste with salt and pepper. Allow to cool slightly.

Step three Cut some baking foil into 4 pieces, and lay a piece of fish in the centre of each foil square and season with salt and pepper. Put a quarter of the tomato mixture on top of each piece of fish, then bring the edges of each square of foil together and scrunch to seal. Put the 4 parcels on a baking sheet and bake for 8 minutes until the cod is opaque and starting to flake. Thick pieces of fish may take 2–3 minutes longer.

Step four Serve the fish with the tomato mixture and any juices from the parcel spooned over the top and garnished with basil leaves.

You can make the tomato mixture in advance and store in the fridge for up to 2 days.

Salmon, prawn and dill lasagne

Ideally we should eat oily fish like salmon twice a week. It's good for the heart and good for the brain so it's worth finding new ways to serve it, such as this tasty lasagne. Suitable for freezing.

Step one Preheat the oven to 200°C/400°F/gas 6.

Step two Melt the butter in a deep saucepan. Add the leek and gently sauté for 5–6 minutes until soft. Add the vinegar, then stir in the flour and cook over the heat until blended. Add the milk, bring to the boil, then stir until thickened. Add the lemon juice, spinach, dill and 50g (2oz) Parmesan. Stir over the heat until the spinach has wilted. Season with salt and black pepper.

Step three Put a third of the salmon, prawns and broccoli into the base of a 21 x 16 x 7cm (8¼ x 6¼ x 2¾in) dish. Pour over a third of the sauce. Place two sheets of lasagne on top. Repeat with more of the fish mixture, sauce and the remaining lasagne sheets, then finish with a layer of the fish mixture and sauce. Sprinkle with the 30g (1oz) Parmesan, then place in the oven for 30 minutes. Leave to stand for 5 minutes before serving.

Serves 4

50g (2oz) butter

1 leek, finely chopped

1½oz (1 tsp) white wine vinegar

50g (2oz) plain flour

600ml (1 pint) milk

2 tbsp fresh lemon juice

100g (3½oz) baby spinach

2 tbsp dill, chopped

80g (2¾oz) Parmesan, grated

300g (10½oz) salmon fillet, skinned and cut into 2-cm (¾-in) cubes

225g (8oz) cooked king prawns

150g (5¼oz) broccoli, sliced into small florets and blanched

4 sheets lasagne

salt and freshly ground black pepper

King prawn stir fry with sugar snap peas

Stir fries are popular, quick and easy meals for the whole family. This particular recipe could also be made with fresh uncooked prawns.

Serves 4

Marinade

1 egg white

1 tsp cornflour

pinch of salt

300g (10½ oz) cooked king prawns (de-veined)

Sauce

375ml (13fl oz) chicken stock

1 tbsp soy sauce

1 tbsp sesame oil

1½ tbsp caster sugar

½ tbsp cider vinegar

1½ tbsp cornflour

2 spring onions, finely sliced

ground white pepper

3 tbsp vegetable oil

2 eggs, lightly beaten

1 garlic clove, crushed

1 onion, thinly sliced

100g (3½ oz) baby corn, cut in half

100g (3½ oz) button mushrooms, cut in half

150g (5¼ oz) sugar snap peas

Step one Lightly beat the egg white and mix it together the cornflour and seasoning. Marinate the prawns in this mixture for about 10 minutes.

Step two To make the sauce, mix together the stock, soy sauce, sesame oil, sugar and vinegar. In a small bowl mix 45ml (3 tbsp) of the sauce with the cornflour until smooth and then stir this into the rest of the sauce. Pour the sauce into a saucepan, bring to the boil and then simmer, stirring, for 2–3 minutes until thickened. Stir in the spring onions and season with a little white pepper.

Step three Strain the marinade from the prawns and discard. Heat 1 tablespoon of the oil in a frying pan and sauté the prawns for about 2 minutes then set aside. Heat another tablespoon of oil in the pan and swirl the beaten egg around to form a thin layer and cook until set. Remove from the pan and fold it over three times like a Swiss roll, cut into strips and set aside.

Step four Add the remaining oil to the pan and sauté the garlic and onion for 2 minutes. Stir-fry the corn, button mushrooms and sugar snap peas for 6 minutes. Add the prawns and the sauce and cook for 2 minutes or until heated through.

Pressed sushi

The Japanese call this type of sushi *oshi sushi*, and it is surprisingly easy to make. This is a fun dish for older children to make.

Step one Put the rice in a pan with the water. Bring up to a boil, cover the pan tightly with a lid, turn down the heat as low as possible and cook for 15 minutes. Turn off the heat and leave to stand for another 15 minutes.

Step two Meanwhile warm the vinegar in a microwave for 10 seconds or warm gently in a pan but do not boil, then stir in the sugar and salt until dissolved.

Step three Line a 20cm (8in) loose-bottomed springform cake tin with two pieces of cling film, allowing plenty of overhang. Lay the smoked salmon on the base of the cake tin, overlapping the slices slightly.

Step four Spoon the cooked rice into a large bowl and stir in the vinegar mixture. Leave the rice to cool for 10 minutes, stirring regularly. Spread the rice over the salmon, fold the cling film over the top of the rice then press the rice down firmly with a potato masher. Chill for 30 minutes.

Step five Lift out the base of the cake tin, unwrap the cling film from the rice side and flip the sushi disc on to a cutting board (salmon-side up). Remove the cling film completely and cut the sushi into pieces with a sharp knife. Serve with soy sauce for dipping.

The sushi will cut more easily if you wet the knife between each cut. Although not suitable for freezing, it can be stored overnight in the fridge wrapped tightly in cling film.

Makes about 32 sushi

250g (9oz) sushi rice
350ml (12fl oz) water
3 tbsp rice wine vinegar
2 tbsp caster sugar
¼ tsp salt
4–6 thin slices smoked salmon
soy sauce for dipping

Marina's spaghetti with seafood

Seafood with spaghetti is one of my favourite meals. If you have some Noilly Prat, this adds a great flavour to the dish. If you have never cooked seafood before, don't worry: it's really very easy and the good news is it takes only minutes. Not suitable for freezing.

Serves 4

500g (1lb) mussels

250g (9oz) clams

2 tbsp olive oil

1 red onion, sliced

1 garlic clove, crushed

50ml (2fl oz) Noilly Prat or white wine (optional)

1 x 400g (14oz) tin chopped tomatoes

100ml (3½ fl oz) fish stock

Tabasco sauce

1 tsp sugar

200g (7oz) spaghetti

250g (9oz) large fresh prawns, peeled, head removed and deveined

1 tbsp chopped fresh basil

1 tbsp fresh lemon juice

salt and freshly ground black pepper

Step one To prepare the mussels and clams: discard any mussels or clams that do not stay closed when gently pressed. Place the mussels and clams in a bowl of salt water for 10 minutes to extract any sand caught in the shells. Only if the mussel or clam shells still feel gritty after the initial soaking do you need to scrub them under a cold running tap using a stiff brush. Use a damp kitchen towel and wipe the shells clean. Remove the beards from the mussels – these are the little fibrous tufts – by cutting them away with a knife or scissors (some cultivated mussels don't have beards). Place the clams and mussels in a colander and give them a final rinse before using them. If you are not using them straight away, store them in the fridge.

Step two Heat the olive oil in a large saucepan and fry the onion and garlic for 7–8 minutes until soft. Add the Noilly Prat or wine, if using, bring to the boil and reduce by half. Add the chopped tomatoes, stock, Tabasco, sugar and salt and black pepper and cook for 10 minutes.

Step three Meanwhile, cook the spaghetti according to the packet instructions. Drain.

Step four Add all the seafood and basil to the tomato sauce, stir well, cover with a lid and cook for 3–4 minutes. Then stir in the cooked spaghetti and lemon juice just before serving.

Krispie fish fingers with lemon mayo dip

Rice Krispies make a tasty coating for fish, and I like to make these finger-sized goujons as they cook quickly and can be easily cooked from frozen. They are not suitable for reheating.

Step one Cut the fish into little finger-sized pieces. Cover and set aside in the fridge.

Step two Put the Rice Krispies, Parmesan and paprika in a food processor, and whizz to fine crumbs. Transfer to a plate, and stir in salt and pepper to taste and the sesame seeds (if using)

Step three Beat the egg in a bowl with a pinch of salt. Spread the flour out on a separate plate. Toss three or four of the fish pieces in the flour then dunk in the egg and roll in the Krispie crumbs until well coated. Place these on a clean plate and continue with the remaining fish.

Step four Cook immediately or freeze (see below for details). Heat the oil in a large frying pan and add the fish fingers. Fry for 1½–2 minutes each side, until golden and cooked through. Transfer to a plate lined with kitchen paper to cool slightly before serving.

Step five To make the dip, mix all of the ingredients together in a small bowl. If you like you can season the dip to taste with a pinch of salt. Serve with the fish fingers.

Another good coating to try is crushed cornflakes. Simply cut the fish into strips, coat in seasoned flour, lightly beaten egg and then crushed cornflakes, and sauté until golden and cooked through.

To freeze, lay the uncooked fish fingers on a baking sheet lined with cling film. Cover with cling film and freeze for around 2 hours, until firm. Transfer to re-sealable plastic bags. Cook directly from frozen as described above (the cooking time is the same).

Serves 6–8

225g (8oz) skinless sole or plaice fillets

45g (1½ oz) Rice Krispies

3 tbsp freshly grated Parmesan

¼ tsp paprika

1 tsp sesame seeds (optional)

1 egg

2 tbsp flour

2–3 tbsp sunflower oil, for frying

salt and pepper, to season

Dip

2 tbsp mayonnaise

2 tbsp thick Greek yoghurt

1 tsp fresh lemon juice

pinch of salt, to season (optional)

Sizzling Asian shrimp

A lot of my more popular recipes for children are Asian-style dishes.

Serves 4

2 tsp sunflower oil

1 tsp grated fresh ginger

1 garlic clove, crushed

340g (12oz) shelled raw tiger prawns (defrosted frozen prawns are fine)

2 tsp sesame oil

2 large or 4 small spring onions, thinly sliced

1 tbsp fresh lime juice

a handful of fresh coriander leaves, to serve (optional)

Step one Heat the sunflower oil in a wok until sizzling. Add the ginger, garlic and prawns and cook for 1–1½ minutes, then turn the prawns and cook for another 1–2 minutes until the prawns have turned pink. Add the sesame oil, spring onions and the lime juice and stir for 30 seconds until fragrant.

Step two Remove from the heat and serve with the coriander leaves scattered over.

It's also good to flavour thin fillets of white fish with garlic, ginger, spring onion and soy sauce and cook them wrapped in foil.

my
KITCHEN
TABLE
For more recipes from My Kitchen Table, sign up for our newsletter at www.mykitchentable.co.uk/newsletter

Mild king prawn curry

This delicious aromatic prawn curry is quick and easy to prepare and is a favourite in my house.

Step one Heat the oil in a large saucepan. Fry the onion, garlic, chilli and red pepper for 5 minutes until almost soft.

Step two Add the garam masala and coat the onion mixture in it, then add the tinned tomatoes, water, creamed coconut, tomato purée and mango chutney. Bring to the boil, cover with a lid, then simmer for 20 minutes.

Step three Add the prawns to the hot sauce and stir over the heat until the prawns turn pink and are cooked through.

Step four Season with salt and pepper and serve with rice, cooked according to the instructions on the packet.

Serves 2–3

1 tbsp sunflower oil

1 large onion, finely chopped

2 garlic cloves, crushed

½ green chilli, finely diced

1 red pepper, deseeded and finely diced

1 tbsp garam masala powder

1 x 400 g tin of chopped tomatoes

360 ml water

50 g (2 oz) creamed coconut

1 tbsp tomato purée

1 tbsp mango chutney

salt and freshly ground black pepper

450g (1 lb) raw king prawns

approx 350g (9 oz) rice

Mini fish pie

I design the menus for one of the largest chains of nurseries in the UK and one of the children's favourite dishes is this fish pie. Another of their favourite recipes is my fruity curried chicken, so it's interesting to see that children often have more sophisticated tastes than we imagine. Making food look attractive is important and so it seems much more appealing to make individual fish pies rather than have a dollop of food on the plate. The pies are suitable for freezing, assembled but unbaked.

Serves 4–6

Potato topping

800g (1¾lb) potatoes

30g (1oz) butter

7 tbsp milk

4 tbsp freshly grated Parmesan

1 egg, lightly beaten

Sauce

45g (1½oz) butter

1 large shallot, diced

2 tbsp white wine vinegar

45g (1½oz) flour

450ml (16fl oz) fish stock

6 tbsp double cream

1½ tsp chopped fresh dill or chives

salt and pepper, to taste

Filling

250g (9oz) salmon

250g (9oz) cod

150g (5½oz) small cooked prawns

70g (2½oz) frozen peas

Step one Preheat the oven to 200°C/400°F/gas 6.

Step two Boil the potatoes in salted water. Drain and mash with the butter, milk and Parmesan and season to taste.

Step three To make the sauce, melt the butter and sauté the shallot for 5–6 minutes until soft. Add the white wine vinegar and boil for 2–3 minutes until the liquid has evaporated. Stir in the flour to make a roux. Gradually, stir in the fish stock and then cook over a medium heat, stirring continuously. Bring to the boil then cook, stirring, until thickened. Remove from the heat and stir in the cream and the chopped dill or chives. Season well as the fish is unseasoned.

Step four Remove the skin from the fish and cut into 2cm (¾in) chunks. Divide all the fish and peas among four or six mini ramekins (depending on the size) and pour over the sauce. If you have time, allow the fish, pea and sauce filling to cool and become less liquid as it is then easier to cover with the mashed potato without it sinking into the filling. Brush the potato topping with a little beaten egg. Bake for 25 minutes.

Sticky salmon and Chinese fried rice

If I was asked to choose just one recipe to encourage a love of eating fish it would be this one. It's funny how the simplest recipes can often be the best.

Step one Place all the ingredients for the marinade in a small saucepan and stir over a gentle heat until the sugar has dissolved. Remove from the heat, pour into an ovenproof dish and leave to cool. Add the cubes of salmon and turn to coat them in the sauce. Leave to marinate for at least one hour.

Step two Cook the rice in a pan of lightly salted boiling water, according to the instructions on the packet, together with the chopped carrots. Four minutes before the end of the cooking time, add the frozen peas. Meanwhile, heat the vegetable oil in a frying pan or wok, beat the egg with a little salt, and pour into the pan, tilting it so that the egg coats the base. Cook until it sets as a thin omelette. Remove from the pan, roll up to form a sausage shape and cut into thin strips and set aside.

Step three Add the butter to the wok and sauté the onion for two minutes. Add the cooked rice mixture, the soy sauce and a little freshly ground black pepper. Stir-fry the rice for about 2 minutes.

Step four Preheat the grill. Place the salmon in a baking tin lined with foil, pour over the marinade and bake for about 5 minutes, turning halfway through and basting occasionally until cooked.

Step five Just before the salmon is ready, stir the strips of egg and spring onion into the rice and heat through. Remove the salmon from the baking tin and serve with rice.

Serves 4

Marinade

1½ tbsp soy sauce

2 tbsp tomato ketchup

1 tbsp white wine vinegar

½ tsp sweet chilli sauce

1½ tbsp dark brown sugar

2 skinned salmon fillets (approx. 800g/7oz), cut into 4cm (1½in) cubes

Chinese fried rice

200g (7oz) basmati rice

65g (2¼oz) carrots, finely chopped

75g (3oz) frozen peas

1 tsp vegetable oil

1 egg, lightly beaten

25g (1oz) butter

65g (2¼oz) onion, finely chopped

2 tbsp soy sauce

1 spring onion, finely sliced

salt and freshly ground black pepper

Fusilli with salmon and spring vegetables

This tasty recipe can be made in less than 20 minutes, and salmon is such a good food to include in your diet as it's rich in essential fatty acids, which are good for the heart, brain and skin. It couldn't be simpler and it's a dish the whole family can enjoy.

Serves 4

200g (7oz) fusilli

2 tbsp light olive oil

1 onion, finely chopped

1 garlic clove, crushed

100g (3½oz) orange pepper cut into strips

100g (3½oz) broccoli florets

1 medium courgette (150g/5¼oz) sliced and then cut into semi-circles

250g (9oz) salmon fillets

250ml (9fl oz) fish stock

150g (5¼oz) crème fraîche (you can use half fat if you prefer)

200ml (7fl oz) vegetable stock

150g (5¼oz) tomatoes, skinned, deseeded and cut into chunks

75g (3oz) Parmesan, grated

salt and freshly ground black pepper

Step one Cook the fusilli according to the directions on the packet.

Step two Heat the olive oil in a heavy-based saucepan and sauté the onion and garlic for 3 minutes, stirring occasionally. Add the orange pepper, broccoli and courgette and sauté for 6–7 minutes stirring occasionally until tender.

Step three Meanwhile cut the salmon into chunks. Put into a saucepan, cover with fish stock and poach over a gentle heat for 3–4 minutes or until cooked. Remove from the pan, strain, break into flakes and set aside.

Step four To make the sauce, stir the crème fraîche and vegetable stock into the cooked vegetables and bring to a simmer. Stir in the chopped tomatoes and chunks of salmon and simmer for 2 minutes, then stir in the Parmesan and season to taste. Toss the drained fusilli with the sauce.

Salmon fishcakes

Yes it is true that fish is good for the brain, so here is a tasty way to be clever. I don't cook the fish before mixing it with the other ingredients as that way it stays lovely and moist. Suitable for freezing.

Step one Boil the unpeeled potatoes in salted water for about 25 minutes until tender (or if you don't have much time, prick the potatoes and cook them in a microwave at 800W for about 10 minutes until soft). Drain and, when cool enough to handle, peel and mash. Mix together with two tablespoons of the mayonnaise, sweet chilli sauce, lemon juice, spring onion, grated Cheddar and ketchup and roughly mash using a potato masher. Mix in the salmon cubes and fresh breadcrumbs and season to taste.

Step two Using your hands, form the mixture into 8 fishcakes. Coat in the dried breadcrumbs. Heat some oil in a large frying pan and sauté for about 5 minutes, turning halfway through, until golden on both sides.

Step three To make the dip, mix together the remaining mayonnaise and sweet chilli sauce.

Makes 8 fishcakes

250g (9oz) potato

5 tbsp mayonnaise

1 tbsp sweet chilli sauce

1 tsp lemon juice

3 spring onions, finely sliced

35g (1¼ oz) Cheddar, grated

2 tbsp tomato ketchup

250g (9oz) raw salmon, cut into small cubes

60g (2¼ oz) fresh breadcrumbs

salt and freshly ground pepper

100g (3½ oz) dried breadcrumbs for coating

sunflower oil, for frying the fish cakes

2 tbsp sweet chilli sauce

Sea bass with ginger and spring onion on a bed of noodles

Sea bass is a delicate fish and the combination of mirin – a sweet rice wine – soy sauce, rice wine vinegar, garlic and ginger gives it a delicious Japanese flavour. Serve on a bed of noodles with beansprouts and sugar snap peas for a special occasion. For adults you can add some chopped red chilli when sautéing the garlic and ginger. Not suitable for freezing.

Serves 4

2 tbsp olive oil

4 sea bass fillets, skin on (approx. 350g/12oz)

2-cm piece of fresh ginger, peeled and thinly sliced

2 garlic cloves

150g (5¼ oz) sugar snap peas, sliced

100g (3½ oz) beansprouts

bunch spring onions, finely sliced

100g (3½ oz) egg noodles

4 tbsp mirin

4 tbsp soy sauce

1 tsp rice wine vinegar

salt and freshly ground black pepper

Step one Heat 1½ tablespoons of the oil in a large frying pan. Season the fish and slash the skin. Fry the fillets for 3–4 minutes, skin-side down over a high heat, until crispy. Turn over and cook for 1 minute. Remove to a plate and keep warm.

Step two Heat the remaining oil. Add the ginger and garlic and fry for 2 minutes. Add the sugar snap peas, beansprouts and half the spring onions and stir-fry for 3 minutes.

Step three Cook the noodles in boiling salted water according to the packet instructions. Drain, then add to the pan with the beansprouts. Season, then mix together the mirin, soy sauce and vinegar.

Step four Pour half of the sauce over the noodles and heat the rest in a small pan. Spoon some noodles onto a plate and place 1 fish fillet on top. Pour over the warm sauce and sprinkle over the remaining spring onions. Serve straight away.

Beef stroganoff with tagliatelle

I buy tail fillet from my butcher to make stroganoff; it's cheaper than normal fillet steak and tastes the same, so it's perfect. Traditionally, you make this with button mushrooms, but chestnut mushrooms are also good, or if you are feeling extravagant you could use shiitake mushrooms. Suitable for freezing (stroganoff only).

Step one Heat 3 teaspoons of the oil in a wok or frying pan. Sauté the mushrooms for 5–6 minutes until golden brown. Transfer to a bowl.

Step two Heat another teaspoon of oil in the pan and fry the steak quickly (about 1–2 minutes) until browned. Don't overcrowd the pan – it is best to cook the meat in 2–3 batches or else the beef will stew in its own juices. Transfer the beef to the bowl with the mushrooms.

Step three Turn down the heat to low. Melt the butter and gently cook the shallots for 8–10 minutes until soft. Add the garlic and thyme and cook for 1 minute. Add the beef stock and boil for 2–3 minutes until reduced by half. Whisk in the cream, mustard, soy sauce and sugar and boil for 2–3 minutes until thick enough to coat the back of a spoon. Reduce the heat to low and add the mushrooms and beef. Season to taste with black pepper and lemon juice (you probably won't need to add salt). Keep warm.

Step four Cook the tagliatelle in a pan of boiling water according to the instructions on the packet. Drain and transfer to plates. Spoon over the sauce. Serve sprinkled with parsley.

Serves 4

1–2 tbsp olive oil

150g (5¼ oz) mushrooms, thinly sliced

225g (8oz) fillet or sirloin steak, thinly sliced

large knob of butter

3 small shallots, thinly sliced

1 garlic clove, crushed

½ tsp thyme leaves

250ml (9fl oz) beef stock

200ml (7fl oz) double cream

½ tsp dijon mustard

2 tsp soy sauce

1 tsp sugar

small squeeze of fresh lemon juice, to taste

200g (7oz) tagliatelle

freshly ground black pepper, to taste

parsley, to serve

Diner's blue plate special meatloaf

A 'blue plate' is a diner's daily special menu item and meatloaf is usually a popular choice. I like mine with a barbecue sauce and plenty of creamy mashed potatoes.

Serves 6–8

1 tbsp olive oil, plus extra for greasing

2 red onions, finely chopped

1 garlic clove, crushed

200ml (7fl oz) tomato ketchup

2 tbsp soft light brown sugar

2 tbsp runny honey or maple syrup

2 tsp Worcestershire sauce

4 tbsp orange juice

85g (3oz) fresh white breadcrumbs (made from about 4 slices of bread, crusts removed)

3 tbsp milk

½ tsp fresh thyme leaves or 1 tsp dried

1 small carrot, grated (45g/1½ oz)

½ apple, peeled, cored and grated (about 75g/3oz)

450g (1lb) lean minced beef

salt and freshly ground black pepper

Step one Preheat the oven to 180°C/350°F/gas 4. Lightly grease a baking sheet.

Step two Heat the oil in a medium saucepan and sauté the onions for 6–8 minutes, until soft. Add the garlic and cook for 1 minute, then transfer half of the onion to a bowl and leave to cool. Add the ketchup, sugar, honey or maple syrup, Worcestershire sauce and orange juice to the saucepan.

Step three Add the breadcrumbs and milk to the onion in the bowl and stir, then add the remaining ingredients and 3 tablespoons of the sauce. Season to taste with salt and pepper, mix together then transfer to the baking sheet and form into a fat log about 20cm (8in) long and 9cm (4in) wide.

Step four Bake the meatloaf for 30 minutes then brush with some of the sauce. Bake for a further 10 minutes, then brush again and bake for 5 minutes. Remove from the oven and leave to rest for 10 minutes.

Step five Meanwhile, heat the remaining sauce until boiling and bubble for 1 minute. Serve the meatloaf in slices with the barbecue sauce.

The meatloaf and sauce can be prepared 1 day ahead and kept in the fridge, covered, until ready to cook.

Fusilli with chipolatas and sweet pepper

You can't go wrong with sausages and pasta. This would be a good dish to make if you have a group of children over as it is so quick and easy to prepare. Suitable for children from 2 years. Not suitable for freezing.

Step one Cook the pasta in boiling salted water according to the instructions on the packet. Drain.

Step two Preheat the oven to 200°C/400°F/gas 6.

Step three Heat the oil and sauté the onion, garlic and peppers for 5 minutes. Meanwhile, cook the sausages in the oven or under a grill. Allow to cool slightly and slice into chunks.

Step four Mix the sausages, pasta, peppers, tomatoes and thyme together. Place in a casserole dish and top with the grated cheese. Bake for 20 minutes.

Serves 4

200g (7oz) fusilli pasta

2 tbsp sunflower oil

150g (5¼ oz) diced onion

5g (¼ oz) chopped garlic

300g (10½ oz) red, yellow and orange peppers, diced

400g (14oz) chipolata sausages (approx. 10)

120g (4¼ oz) cherry tomatoes, cut into halves

leaves picked from 1 small bunch of thyme

50g (2oz) Cheddar, grated

Annabel's tasty burgers

These burgers can be made with beef, lamb or chicken. You can serve them in a toasted bun with extras like lettuce, pickled cucumber, sliced tomato, thinly sliced sautéd onion and maybe a little ketchup or mustard.

Makes 10 burgers

1 tbsp vegetable oil

1 onion, peeled and finely chopped

450g (1lb) lean minced beef or lamb

1 tbsp freshly chopped parsley (optional)

1 beef stock cube, finely crumbled

1 apple, peeled and grated

½ egg, lightly beaten

60g (2¼ oz) fresh breadcrumbs

½ tbsp Worcestershire sauce

salt and freshly ground black pepper

a little flour

a little margarine and Marmite (optional) if grilling

Step one Heat the vegetable oil in a pan and fry the onion for about 5 minutes or until softened. Set aside to cool down. Gently squeeze some of the juice from the grated apples using your hands. In a mixing bowl, combine the sautéd onion together with all the other ingredients. With floured hands, form into 10 burgers.

Step two Dot each burger with a little margarine and Marmite (if you like) and cook the burgers under a preheated grill for about 4 minutes each side. Alternatively, heat some vegetable oil in a frying pan and sauté the burgers over a high heat to begin with to seal them and then lower the heat and cook for about 4 minutes each side.

Nicholas' multi-layered cottage pie

You can either make one large cottage pie or make several individual ones in ramekin dishes to freeze for use later.

Step one Peel and chop the swede and carrots and cook in boiling, lightly salted water for 20 minutes, or until tender, then mash with the knob of butter until smooth.

Step two Heat half a tablespoon of the oil in a large, non-stick frying pan and sauté the minced beef for 7–8 minutes or until any liquid has evaporated. Remove the beef from the pan then set aside. Heat the remaining oil in a fairly large casserole dish and sauté the onion and leek for 3 minutes. Add the red pepper and sauté for 2 minutes, then add the mushrooms and sauté for 4 minutes. Add the tomatoes and sauté for 3 minutes. Return the cooked mince to the pan together with the tomato purée, Worcestershire sauce, herbs, bay leaf and beef stock and simmer for about 30 minutes. Season to taste.

Step three Meanwhile, peel and chop the potatoes, boil for 15–20 minutes, then drain. Return the cooked potatoes to the empty saucepan and mash together with butter, milk, salt and pepper until smooth.

Step four Preheat the grill to high. Place the mashed carrots and swede in the base of an 18cm (7in) diameter, 7.5cm (3in) deep ovenproof glass dish. Arrange the meat on top, then cover with a layer of cooked peas and top with a layer of potato. Brush the potato with the beaten egg and grill for 3–4 minutes, or until the top is browned.

Serves 6

250g (9oz) swede,
200g (7oz) carrots
generous knob of butter
2½ tbsp vegetable oil
450g (1lb) minced beef
1 large onion, finely chopped
100g (3½ oz) leek, finely chopped
100g (3½ oz) red pepper, finely chopped
150g (5½ oz) button mushrooms, diced
1 medium tomatoes, skinned, deseeded and chopped
1 tbsp tomato purée
2 tsp Worcestershire sauce
½ tsp dried mixed herbs
1 bay leaf
1 beef stock cube dissolved in 350ml (12¼ fl oz) boiling water
675g (1½ lb) potatoes
50g (2oz) unsalted butter
6 tbsp milk
salt and white and black pepper
225g (8oz) frozen peas, cooked
1 beaten egg

Annabel's Bolognese

This tasty sauce has hidden vegetables blended in, so it's great for fussy eaters.

Serves 4

3 tbsp vegetable oil

150g (5¼ oz) onion, finely chopped

1 garlic clove, crushed

50g (2oz) carrot, grated

100g (3½ oz) button mushrooms, sliced

1 beef stock cube dissolved in 300ml (½ pint) boiling water

250g (9oz) minced lean beef

300ml (½ pint) passata

1 tbsp tomato ketchup

½ tbsp Worcestershire sauce

1 tsp brown sugar

½ tsp dried oregano

1 bay leaf

200g (7oz) spaghetti

salt and freshly ground black pepper

Step one Heat half the vegetable oil in a saucepan, add half the onion and sauté for 2 minutes, stirring occasionally. Add half the crushed garlic and sauté for a few seconds. Add the carrot and mushrooms and cook for 3 minutes. Transfer to a blender, stir in half the beef stock and blitz until smooth.

Step two Meanwhile, heat the remaining oil in a saucepan, add the remaining onion and sauté for 2 minutes. Add the rest of the garlic and sauté for a few seconds. Add the minced beef and sauté, stirring occasionally for 7–8 minutes. Add the remaining stock, passata, tomato ketchup, Worcestershire sauce, brown sugar, oregano and bay leaf. Stir in the carrot and mushroom mixture and simmer, covered, for about 30 minutes. Remove the bay leaf. Season to taste. Keep warm.

Step three Cook the spaghetti according to the instructions on the packet, drain and toss with the Bolognese sauce.

Veal escalopes with tomato and basil sauce

This is suitable for children from 18 months. Not suitable for freezing.

Step one Heat 1 tablespoon of olive oil in a saucepan. Add the onion and garlic and sauté for 2–3 minutes. Add the tinned tomatoes, purées, sugar and thyme. Bring to the boil, cover with a lid and simmer for 20 minutes. Whizz the sauce to a purée using a hand blender.

Step two Cook the pasta according to the instructions on the packet. Drain and add to the sauce with the basil. Keep warm.

Step three Mix together the breadcrumbs, Parmesan and parsley. If necessary, cover the veal with clingfilm and bash it out to a thickness of about 4mm using a mallet. Season the veal and coat in flour, then dip into the beaten egg. Coat the veal in the breadcrumbs. Heat the remaining oil in a large non-stick frying pan. Fry the veal for 1½–2 minutes on both sides until golden and just cooked through. Remove from the heat and rest for 2 minutes.

Step four Spoon some spaghetti onto a plate and serve with the veal on top.

Serves 4

Tomato sauce
3 tbsp olive oil
1 onion, chopped
2 garlic cloves, crushed
2 x 400g (14oz) tins chopped tomatoes
1 tbsp tomato purée
1 tbsp sundried tomato purée
1 tsp sugar
½ tsp dried thyme or 1 tsp fresh thyme
3 tbsp fresh basil, chopped
250g (9oz) spaghetti
150g (5½oz) fresh white breadcrumbs
30g (1oz) Parmesan, finely grated
2 tbsp parsley, chopped
2 tbsp flour, to coat the veal
4 thin veal escalopes (about 00–100g/ 0–0½ oz each)
2 eggs, beaten
salt and freshly ground black pepper

Hungarian goulash

My mother used to make a version of this for me when I was a child and I loved it. Mine has a little bit of a kick, but you can use less cayenne pepper if you prefer. It is delicious served with noodles or rice. Suitable for freezing.

Serves 6

2 tbsp flour, for coating

450g (1lb) lean braising steak, cut into cubes

vegetable oil for frying

2 large onions, finely sliced

1 red pepper, deseeded and cut into strips

½ green pepper, deseeded and cut into strips

1 garlic clove, crushed

2 tsp smoked Spanish paprika

½ tsp cayenne pepper

2 x 400g (14oz) tins chopped tomatoes, drained

2 tbsp tomato purée

300ml (10½ fl oz) beef stock

2 tbsp chopped fresh parsley

3 tbsp soured cream or yoghurt

salt and freshly ground black pepper

Step one Preheat the oven to 150°C/300°F/gas 2.

Step two Season the flour with a little salt and pepper and roll the beef cubes in it. Fry them in the oil in 2 batches until browned on all sides.

Step three Meanwhile, sauté the onions for about 10 minutes until soft. Add the peppers and cook these for 5 minutes. Add the garlic, sprinkle over the paprika and cayenne pepper and continue to cook for about 2 minutes.

Step four Put the meat and vegetables into a casserole dish and add all the remaining ingredients except the parsley and soured cream. Cover and cook in the oven for 1¾ hours, stirring occasionally. Finally, stir in the parsley and soured cream before serving.

Sesame beef stir fry

Provided you are not vegetarian, it is important to include red meat in your child's diet, as red meat provides the richest source of iron and iron deficiency is the most common nutritional deficiency in children in the UK. This recipe is a firm family favourite in my house. I usually make it using tail fillet cut into thin strips, which is slightly cheaper but has exactly the same taste and soft texture of proper fillet steak.

Step one Heat the sesame oil in a wok and stir-fry the garlic, carrots, sweetcorn and courgette for 3–4 minutes. Add the beef and continue to stir-fry for 4–5 minutes.

Step two Mix the cornflour together with 1 tablespoon of water and stir into the beef stock. Stir this into the pan together with the sugar, soy sauce, Tabasco and sesame seeds. Bring to the simmer, cook until slightly thickened and serve with rice.

Serves 4

1 tbsp sesame oil

1 garlic clove, crushed

1 medium carrot, cut into matchsticks

100g (3½ oz) baby sweetcorn, cut into quarters

1 courgette (approx. 100g/3½oz), cut into matchsticks

300g (10¼ oz) beef fillet, or rump steak, cut into very fine strips

1 tbsp cornflour

150ml (5¼ fl oz) beef stock

2 tbsp dark brown sugar

2 tbsp soy sauce

few drops of Tabasco sauce

1 tbsp sesame seeds

Lloyd's leg of lamb

This is absolutely delicious on a barbecue in summer but also works well in the oven. The lamb is also good eaten cold the next day. Ask your butcher to butterfly a leg of lamb for you – you will end up with a boned, flattened cut of lamb that is easy to carve and takes much less time to cook. This can be served with couscous mixed with some diced roasted vegetables like aubergine, courgette, onion and sweet pepper.

Serves 6

Marinade

150ml (¼ pint) oil

30ml (2 tbsp) walnut oil

150ml (¼ pint) red wine

1 tsp oregano

60ml (4 tbsp) fresh lemon juice

2 or 3 garlic cloves, crushed

2 tbsp chopped parsley

1 tsp sea salt

¼ teaspoon ground black pepper

1½ kg (3¼ lb) leg of lamb, boned and butterflied

Step one Mix all the ingredients for the marinade together. Trim away as much excess fat from the lamb as you can. Pierce the lamb all over with the sharp point of a knife and place in a large polythene bag together with the marinade. Tie up the bag and leave in the fridge for 12–24 hours, turning frequently until ready to cook.

Step two Barbecue over indirect heat until cooked through. Alternatively, preheat the oven to 180°C/350°F/gas 4. Place the lamb on a rack over a roasting tin and roast in the oven for between 40 minutes and 1 hour depending on its weight and how you like it cooked. Take the lamb out of the oven and let it rest under foil for 15–20 minutes before carving across the grain into slices.

Have you made this recipe? Tell us what you think at
www.mykitchentable.co.uk/blog

Stir-fried beef with noodles

This is one of my favourite recipes, which is loved by my children and often requested by them when I ask what they would like for supper. This sauce has a lovely rich Japanese-style flavour.

Step one Cut the beef across the grain into thin slices, then stack a few slices on top of each other and cut into slivers the size of long matchsticks. Whisk the eggs with the cornflour and a pinch of salt to make a batter. Add the meat. Stir well to coat. Slice the carrot and courgettes and cut them into matchsticks.

Step two Fill a large wok a quarter full of oil and when the oil is just beginning to smoke, add the carrot and courgette and stir-fry for 1 minute. Remove and transfer to a dish lined with paper towels.

Step three Reheat the oil and when it is starting to smoke, add half the beef, using tongs to make sure the strips of beef remain separate. Fry until crispy, about 3–5 minutes, then drain and add to the carrot and courgettes. Repeat with the remaining beef.

Step four Clean out the wok, add 1 tablespoon of oil, and when hot add the spring onions, chilli and garlic. Stir fry for a few seconds, then add the cooked noodles.

Step five Make the sauce by mixing the rice vinegar and soy sauce with the cornflour and stock and add the caster sugar. Add to the noodles, then toss with the beef and cooked vegetables. Stir-fry briefly until heated through.

If you freeze the beef for 1 hour it will make slicing it easier.

Serves 4

300g (10½ oz) sirloin, rump or fillet steak

2 eggs

4 level tbsp cornflour

pinch of salt

1 medium carrot, peeled

2 medium courgettes, peeled

sunflower oil

4 spring onions, sliced

1 red chilli, deseeded and chopped

1 garlic clove, peeled and crushed

100g (3½ oz) medium egg noodles, cooked according to the instructions on the packet

Sauce

3 tbsp rice vinegar

2 tbsp soy sauce

1 tsp cornflour

3 tbsp chicken stock or water

2 tbsp caster sugar

Pork and beef meatballs with tagine sauce

This serves as a tasty meal that the whole family can enjoy. Children often have more sophisticated tastes than adults imagine. Suitable for freezing.

Serves 4

Tagine sauce

1 tbsp oil

1 small onion, finely chopped

150g (5½ oz) butternut squash, coarsely grated

½ tsp fresh ginger, grated

½ tsp garam masala

½ tsp ground cinnamon

½ tsp ground coriander

1 x 400g (14oz) tin chopped tomatoes

250ml (9fl oz) chicken stock

1 tsp sundried tomato purée

1 tsp honey

Meatballs

125g (4½ oz) pork mince

125g (4½ oz) beef mince

30g (1oz) fresh breadcrumbs

15g (½ oz) Parmesan, grated

½ tsp chopped fresh coriander

1 egg yolk

200g (7oz) pasta

Step one First make the tagine sauce. Heat the oil in a saucepan and add the onion and butternut squash. Sauté for 5 minutes, then add the ginger. Add the spices and fry for 1 minute. Add the remaining ingredients. Season and simmer for 10 minutes until the onion and squash are soft. Blend using a hand blender until smooth. Pour back into the saucepan.

Step two To make the meatballs, put all of the ingredients into a bowl. Season and mix together, then shape into 20 balls. Bring the sauce to the boil, then drop in the meatballs in a single layer. Cover and simmer for 15 minutes.

Step three Meanwhile, cook the pasta according to the instructions on the packet. Drain. Serve the meatballs with the pasta.

Spaghetti with pesto

Adding parsley to the mixture helps to give a good green colour. You could add a few chopped sunblush tomatoes to the spaghetti, too, or sprinkle with some pine nuts. The pesto sauce is suitable for freezing for up to 2 months.

Step one Toast the pine nuts in a frying pan until lightly golden. Remove from the pan and leave to cool.

Step two Cook the spaghetti in a large pan of lightly salted boiling water according to the instructions on the packet.

Step three Meanwhile, tip the Parmesan, garlic, parsley, basil, sugar and cooled pine nuts into a food-processor and whizz until finely chopped. Slowly add the olive oil while the motor is running. Add the water and season. Spoon into a small bowl.

Step four Drain the cooked pasta and put it back into the saucepan. Add 4–5 tablespoons of pesto and toss together. Sprinkle with extra Parmesan before serving.

Serves 4

225g (8oz) spaghetti

Pesto sauce

50g (2oz) pine nuts

50g (2oz) Parmesan, grated, plus extra for serving

1–2 garlic cloves

small bunch of parsley leaves

small bunch of basil leaves and stalks

pinch of sugar

100ml (3½ fl oz) olive oil

1 tbsp water

salt and freshly ground black pepper

Spinach, ricotta and tomato lasagne

This is a big, hearty family dish that is suitable for freezing.

Serves 6

9 sheets no precook or fresh lasagne

Tomato sauce

2 tbsp olive oil

1 large onion, peeled and chopped

1 garlic clove, crushed

1 tbsp balsamic vinegar

2 x 400g (14oz) tins chopped tomatoes

4 tbsp sunblush tomatoes, chopped

2 tbsp tomato purée

Spinach and ricotta filling

1 tbsp olive oil

½ small onion

500g (18oz) fresh spinach, washed and tough stalks removed

250g (9oz) ricotta cheese

6 tbsp freshly grated Parmesan

salt and freshly ground black pepper

Cheese sauce

30g (1oz) butter

30g (1oz) plain flour

450ml (16fl oz) milk

75g (3oz) Gruyère

salt and freshly ground black pepper

Step one Preheat the oven to 180°C/350°F/gas 4.

Step two To make the tomato sauce, heat the oil in a pan and sauté the onion and garlic for 4 minutes. Add the balsamic vinegar and cook for about 30 seconds. Drain half the juice from the cans of chopped tomatoes and add the tomatoes, sunblush tomatoes and tomato purée. Bring to the boil and simmer for 10 minutes.

Step three Meanwhile, make the filling. Heat the oil in another pan and sauté the onion for 4 minutes until softened. Stir in the spinach and cook until wilted, then squeeze out the excess water. Mix with the ricotta cheese and 2 tablespoons of the Parmesan and chop for a few seconds in a food processor. Season with a little salt and pepper. Set aside.

Step four For the cheese sauce, melt the butter, stir in the flour and cook for about 1 minute. Gradually stir in the milk and cook for about 2 minutes until thickened. Grate the Gruyère and stir this is in until melted. Season to taste.

Step five If you are using fresh lasagne, cook it in boiling lightly salted water first, according to the instructions on the packet. To assemble the lasagne, spoon a third of the tomato sauce on the base of a 24 x 19 x 7cm (9.5 x 7.5 x 2.75in) dish and cover with a layer of the spinach and ricotta mixture. Cover with 3 sheets of lasagne followed by a layer of tomato sauce. Repeat with each layer twice, finishing off with a layer of the cheese sauce. Sprinkle over the remaining Parmesan and bake in the oven for 30 minutes.

Spaghetti primavera

You can make this with spaghetti or tagliatelle. The sauce is very simple and quick to prepare. You can use other vegetables like carrot sticks or cauliflower florets depending on what your child likes. To preserve the vitamin C content of the vegetables, cook them in the minimum amount of water until they are just tender.

Step one Cook the spaghetti according to the instructions on the packet. Blanch the broccoli and courgette in lightly salted boiling water for 4 minutes.

Step two Melt the butter in a saucepan and gently fry the spring onions for 1–2 minutes. Stir in the peas and cook for 1 minute. Stir in the chopped tomato and the blanched broccoli and courgette and cook for 1 minute more. Stir in the crème fraîche, vegetable stock, squeeze of lemon juice and Parmesan. Cook over a gentle heat for 2–3 minutes. Season to taste then stir in the cooked spaghetti.

Serves 3

150g (5oz) spaghetti

100g (4oz) broccoli, cut into small florets

75g (3oz) courgette, cut into strips

15g (½oz) butter

4 spring onions, finely sliced

100g (4oz) frozen peas

1 tomato (approx. 140g/5oz), skinned, deseeded and chopped

150ml (5¼ fl oz) crème fraîche

75ml (2⅓ fl oz) vegetable stock

squeeze of fresh lemon juice

4 tbsp freshly grated Parmesan

salt and freshly ground black pepper

Summer risotto

I like to make my risotto in a large frying pan. You will need to add the liquid to the rice little by little, waiting to add more until all the liquid has been absorbed and stirring frequently. It usually takes about 30 minutes to prepare, depending on your pan and your stove. Stir in a little extra stock if you need to re-heat the risotto.

Serves 4–6

900ml (1½ pints) vegetable stock

4 large shallots or one onion, finely chopped

1 garlic clove, crushed

40g (1½ oz) butter

1 tbsp olive oil

50g (2oz) red pepper

200g (7oz) arborio (risotto) rice

75g (3oz) courgette, diced

2 medium tomatoes, skinned, deseeded and chopped (approx. 225g/8oz)

4 tbsp white wine

40g (1½ oz) Parmesan, shaved

Step one Bring the stock to the boil and allow to simmer. Heat the oil and butter in a large frying pan and sauté the shallots and garlic for 1 minute. Add the red pepper and cook for 5 minutes, stirring occasionally until softened.

Step two Add the rice and make sure that it is well coated. Stir for 1 minute. Add 1 or 2 ladlefuls of hot stock and simmer, stirring, until it has been absorbed, then add another ladleful of stock. Continue adding the stock a little at a time and simmer until the rice absorbs the liquid before adding more, stirring frequently. After 10 minutes, add the diced courgette and tomato. After about 8 minutes add the white wine. When all the stock has been added and the rice is cooked (it will probably take about 20 minutes for the rice to cook through), stir in the Parmesan until melted and season to taste.

KITCHEN TABLE

Have you made this recipe? Tell us what you think at www.mykitchentable.co.uk/blog

Butternut squash gratin with penne

Butternut squash is rich in betacarotene and it tastes delicious mixed with a cheese sauce and pasta then baked in the oven with a golden breadcrumb topping. Suitable for children from 1 year. Suitable for freezing.

Step one Preheat the oven to 200°C/400°F/gas 6.

Step two Cut the squash into 2cm pieces. Steam for 8 minutes.

Step three Cook the pasta in boiling salted water according to the packet instructions and drain. Meanwhile make the sauce. Melt the butter, add the flour and mix over the heat for about a minute. Gradually blend in the milk, then bring to the boil, stir until thickened and then lower the heat, add the double cream and cook for a minute. Remove from the heat and stir in the Parmesan until melted. Season with the nutmeg.

Step four Mix the penne, squash, cheese sauce and sage together. Pour into a dish. Sprinkle with the breadcrumbs and Gruyère. Bake in the preheated oven for 25 minutes.

Serves 4

350g (12¼ oz) butternut squash (peeled weight)

175g (6oz) penne

Sauce

30g (1oz) butter

30g (1oz) flour

450ml (¾ pint) milk

4 tbsp double cream

75g (3oz) Parmesan, grated

pinch nutmeg

2 tbsp sage, chopped

60g (2¼ oz) breadcrumbs

55g (2¼ oz) Gruyère, grated

Hidden vegetable tomato sauce

This is a great way to get children to eat vegetables. There are six vegetables blended into the tomato sauce and what they can't see, they can't pick out.

Serves 4

2 tbsp light olive oil

1 medium onion, peeled and finely chopped

1 garlic clove, crushed

50g (2oz) carrots, peeled and grated

50g (2oz) courgettes, grated

50g (2oz) butternut squash, peeled and grated

50g (2oz) button mushrooms, sliced

1 tbsp balsamic vinegar

500g (1lb 2oz) passata

2 tbsp tomato purée

1 tsp soft brown sugar

200ml (7fl oz) vegetable stock

½ tsp dried oregano

1 bay leaf

handful of torn basil leaves (optional)

salt and freshly ground black pepper

Step one Heat the oil in a saucepan and cook the onion on a low heat for 7–8 minutes. Add the garlic and cook for 1 minute. Add the grated carrot, courgette, butternut squash and sliced mushrooms and cook for 4 minutes, stirring occasionally. Add the balsamic vinegar and cook for 1 minute.

Step two Add the passata, tomato paste, sugar, stock, dried oregano, bay leaf and basil (if using). Cook, uncovered, over a low heat for about 35–40 minutes. Remove the bay leaf, transfer to a blender and blitz until smooth. Season to taste.

Caramelised onion and Gruyère tart

This is my favourite recipe for quiche and the slow cooking of the onions gives them a delicious flavour. The pastry takes only a few minutes to make in a food processor, but you could use bought shortcrust pastry instead.

Step one Put the flour, salt and mustard powder in a food-processor and process until the mixture resembles soft breadcrumbs. Gradually add the egg and enough water to form a good consistency. Press into a ball with your hands and chill in the fridge for at least 30 minutes.

Step two Preheat the oven to 220°C /425°F/gas 7.

Step three To make the filling, heat the vegetable oil and the butter in a large frying pan and sauté the onions over a fairly high heat for about 5 minutes. Add the thyme leaves about 3 minutes before the end of the cooking time for the onions. Lower the heat and cook for a further 20 minutes, cover with non-stick baking paper, and stir occasionally until the onions are caramelised. Season with a little salt. Lightly beat the eggs, stir in the milk and the grated Gruyère. Season with a little pepper and stir in the caramelised onions.

Step four Grease a deep, loose-bottomed flan tin. On a lightly floured work surface, roll out the dough and line the base and sides of the flan tin. Prick the base of the pastry and bake blind in the oven for 10 minutes. Remove the baking paper and the beans, turn down the temperature to 190°C/375°F/gas 5 and cook for a further 5 minutes. Spoon the onion mixture into the flan case and sprinkle with the Parmesan. Bake in the oven for 20–25 minutes.

Serves 8

Pastry
225g (8oz) plain flour
pinch of salt
½ tsp mustard powder
1 egg
1 tbsp water

Filling
1 tbsp vegetable oil
15g (½ oz) butter
500g (1lb 2oz) onions, thinly sliced
2 tsp thyme leaves
4 eggs
300ml (½ pint) milk
150g (5¼ oz) Gruyère, grated
25g (1oz) Parmesan, grated
salt and freshly ground black pepper

Ratatouille omelette

This concoction of sautéd Mediterranean vegetables mixed with eggs and topped with grated cheese in the style of a Spanish omelette is quite delicious and a meal in itself.

Serves 6

1 small onion, sliced

3 tbsp olive oil

1 aubergine, sliced

1 large courgette, sliced

1 red pepper, cored, deseeded and cut into strips

2 tomatoes, skinned, deseeded and chopped

6 eggs

30ml (2 tbsp) cold water

25g (1oz) butter

75ml (3fl oz) double cream

75g (3oz) Gruyère, grated

salt and freshly ground black pepper

Step one Gently sauté the onion in olive oil in a heavy-based frying pan until soft. Add the aubergine, courgette, pepper and tomatoes, cover the pan for a further 5 minutes. Season to taste.

Step two Preheat the grill. Lightly whisk the eggs with the cold water, then mix in the cooked vegetables. Heat the butter in the pan. When the butter is frothy, pour in the egg mixture and cook until set. Remove from the heat, pour over the double cream and cover with the grated cheese. Cook under the grill for a few minutes until golden. Leave the handle of the frying pan sticking out of the grill and cover with aluminum foil if necessary.

Potato pizzette bites

Slices of crisp potato make an unusual base for small finger-sized pizzas or pizzette. I always have some handy home made tomato sauce ready in the freezer for quick bites like this.

Step one Preheat the oven to 200°C/400°F/gas 6.

Step two Cut eight large slices of potato, cutting crosswise from the centre of the potato, each around 2mm/⅛in thick. You won't need the thinner end bits of the potato, but these will keep for up to 2 days in the fridge, covered with cold water, and can be used for mashed or boiled potatoes.

Step three Brush each potato slice with oil and season with a little salt and pepper. Lay the slices on a baking sheet lined with non-stick baking parchment and bake for 10 minutes. Turn the slices over and bake for a further 8-10 minutes, until golden and crisp. Watch carefully for the last 2-3 minutes.

Step four Top each potato slice with around one teaspoon of tomato sauce and scatter over the cheese. Bake for a further 5-7 minutes, or grill for 2-3 minutes, until the cheese has melted. Cool slightly before serving.

Serves 2 (easily doubled)

1 large waxy-type potato, skin on and thoroughly washed (Desirée, or similar)

1 tbsp olive oil

3 tbsp Tomato Sauce (see page 116)

50g (2oz) Cheddar or mozzarella, grated

salt and freshly ground black pepper, to season

Vegetable tempura

Crisp tempura batter is usually a good way to tempt sworn veggie-haters to have a taste. To keep the batter light, mix it as quickly as possible and don't worry if there are a few lumps.

Serves 4

For the dipping sauce

2 tbsp mirin

1 tbsp soy sauce

1 tbsp water

½ tsp sugar

½ red pepper, deseeded and cut into thin strips

1 small yellow or green courgette, cut into ½-cm (about ¼-in) thick rounds

1 small head broccoli, broken into bite-sized florets

handful of mangetout, trimmed

450ml (15fl oz) vegetable oil, for deep frying

100g (3½ oz) flour

50g (2oz) cornflour

250ml (9fl oz) sparkling water or soda water

Step one Stir the dipping sauce ingredients together until the sugar has dissolved. Divide among four small dipping bowls.

Step two Have all of the vegetables prepared before you make the batter. You can prepare them a couple of hours in advance and keep them on a plate in the fridge, covered with a damp piece of kitchen paper and then wrapped with cling film.

Step three Put the oil in a large, deep pan (it should not come more than halfway up the side of the pan) or deep fat fryer. Heat the oil to 190°C/375°F. Line a couple of baking sheets with a double layer of kitchen paper.

Step four Put the flour and cornflour in a large bowl and mix together with a fork. Add the sparkling water and mix quickly with the fork – don't worry if there are a few lumps. The batter should be the consistency of single cream; if it is too thick, add an extra 1 or 2 tablespoons of water. Drop 5 or 6 pieces of the prepared vegetables into the batter then gently put them one by one into the hot oil. Don't overcrowd the pan or the oil will get too cold and the batter will be greasy. Fry for 2–3 minutes, turning once, until puffed and crisp and turning slightly golden at the edges. Use a slotted spoon to transfer the cooked vegetables to the baking sheets and let them drain for 1–2 minutes. Meanwhile continue dipping and cooking the remainder of the vegetables.

You can also test the heat of the oil by dropping a cube of bread into the oil – if it is the correct temperature the bread should turn golden brown in around 20 seconds.

Tempura is best eaten within a few minutes of being cooked, but can be kept warm in an oven preheated to 120°C/250°F/ gas ¼ for 10–15 minutes.

Mini muffin pizzas

These mini pizzas are delicious. I have used a courgette and cherry tomato topping but you can choose any topping, perhaps adding some pitted olives on top of the tomato sauce before covering with the grated cheese.

Step one Heat the olive oil in a small saucepan and sauté the onion and garlic for 3–4 minutes. Add the passata, together with the tomato purée and seasoning and cook for approximately 2 minutes or until the mixture is thick enough to spread. Remove from the heat and stir in the torn basil leaves, if using.

Step two Toast the split muffins or focaccia bread and divide the tomato sauce between them. Choose your favourite topping and then cover with the grated cheese. Place under a preheated grill until golden and bubbling.

Makes 4 mini pizzas

1 tbsp olive oil

½ small onion, finely chopped (approx. 60g/2oz)

1 small garlic clove, crushed

100ml (3½ fl oz) passata

½ tbsp tomato purée

pinch of sugar

pinch of salt and pepper

1 tbsp fresh basil leaves, torn into pieces (optional)

Toppings

sweetcorn

sweet pepper

mushrooms

sliced pitted olives

cherry tomatoes

basil or preferred herbs

75g (3oz) grated Cheddar or mozzarella cheese, or a mixture of both

2 English muffins or some focaccia bread, halved

Healthy salad kebabs

These can be savoury or sweet. For the sticks you can use bamboo skewers or thin plastic straws. Here are some suggestions for food combinations to thread onto the skewers.

Makes as many as you like!

Savoury kebabs

slices of ham or turkey rolled up and interspersed with cubes of cheese and wedges of pineapple

cherry tomatoes and mozzarella cheese

cucumber, carrot, red pepper and cubes of Gruyère or Emmenthal

chicken tikka pieces with cucumber

Fruit kebabs

chunks of pineapple

dried apricots

strawberries

melon balls or melon slices and prosciutto

kiwi

grapes

mango chunks.

Balsamic dip

1 tbsp olive oil

1 tsp balsamic vinegar

½ tsp honey

salt and freshly ground black pepper to season

Step one Simply choose your ingredients from the list on the left and place them in bowls, then thread them onto the skewers to serve.

Step two To make the balsamic dip, whisk together the ingredients, season to taste, then serve in small bowls. This dip goes well with the tomato and mozzarella, and the prosciutto and melon kebabs.

Tomato soup

A lovely rich tomato soup, which contains four differen[t]
fresh thyme and basil add a beautiful flavour to the sou[p]

Step one Heat the oil and sauté the onion, pepper, carrot
and celery. Cook for 5 minutes. Add the garlic, the chopped
tomatoes, then the tomato purée, sugar, thyme and stock. Bring
to the boil and simmer covered with a lid for 25–30 minutes.
Whizz until smooth. Season to taste and stir in the cream and
basil.

Serves 4

1 tbsp olive oil

1 small red onion,
peeled and chopped

½ red pepper, diced

1 small carrot, grated

½ stick celery

1 clove garlic, crushed

1 x 400g (14oz) tin
chopped tomatoes

2 tbsp tomato purée

½ tsp sugar

1 tsp fresh thyme
leaves

300ml (½ pint)
vegetable stock

2–3 tbsp double cream

salt and freshly ground
black pepper

few basil leaves,
shredded

For a video masterclass on chopping an onion, go to
www.mykitchentable.co.uk/videos/choppingonion

a's lovely onion soup

My daughter Lara loves onion soup and this one has a delicious flavour, as I allow the onions to caramelise to bring out their flavour. You can mix ordinary onions with red onions if you like. It's great comfort food on a cold winter's night.

Serves 8

30ml (2 tbsp) olive oil

50g (2oz) butter

550g (1¼ lb) onions, thinly sliced

1 garlic clove, crushed

½ tsp granulated sugar

1.2 litres (2 pints) good beef stock

1 large potato, peeled and cubed

150ml (¼ pint) dry white wine

½ French loaf

75g (3oz) Gruyère, grated

salt and freshly ground black pepper

Step one Melt the oil and butter in a large casserole. Add the onions, garlic and sugar, and cook over a medium heat, stirring until the onions have browned. Reduce the heat to the lowest setting, cover the onions with a sheet of non-stick baking paper and leave the onions to cook slowly for 30 minutes.

Step two Meanwhile, put 600ml (1 pint) of the stock into a saucepan, add the chopped potato and cook for 10–12 minutes or until the potato is soft. Blend the potato with some of the stock in a food processor or blender. This will help to thicken the soup.

Step three Remove the non-stick baking paper and pour the thickened stock, the remaining beef stock and the wine over the caramelised onions. Season, then stir with a wooden spoon, scraping the base of the pan to get the full flavour of the caramelized onions. Simmer gently uncovered for 30 minutes.

Step four To make the cheesey French bread slices to float on top of the soup, first cut the loaf diagonally into 12mm (½in) slices and toast lightly on both sides. Pour the soup into individual oven-proof bowls and top each one with a slice of bread. Sprinkle the bread liberally with the grated cheese. Place the bowls under a hot grill until the cheese is melted and bubbling. Serve immediately.

Chicken and corn chowder

My three children love this soup and it's very quick and easy to prepare and a complete meal in one bowl. It would also be good to include this in a flask in your child's lunchbox when the weather gets cold. Suitable for freezing.

Step one Melt the butter in a large saucepan and sauté the shallot for 5 minutes, until soft. Add the potato, corn and stock, bring to a simmer and cook until the potato is soft. Blend half of this mixture until smooth, then return to the pan and stir in the double cream. Season to taste

Step two Stir in the shredded chicken. Serve with a little chopped parsley scattered over if wanted.

Serves 4

15g (1 tbsp) butter

1 large shallot (55g/2oz), finely chopped

1 medium potato (e.g. Desirée), about 200g/7oz, peeled and diced into 1cm cubes

1 x 400g (14oz) (or 2 x 198g) tin Green Giant sweetcorn, drained

650ml (1 pint 2fl oz) good chicken stock

6 tbsp double cream

50g/2oz shredded, cooked chicken

1 tbsp chopped parsley (optional), to serve

Turkey pasta salad

A quick and easy salad that is very nutritious. Great for lunchboxes or a light snack. This has a really nice dressing that children love!

Serves 2–3

50g (2oz) pasta shapes

50g (1½ oz) broccoli florets

100g (3½ oz) turkey or chicken breast fillet, cooked and chopped

100g (3½ oz) tinned or frozen sweetcorn

2 tomatoes, skinned, deseeded and chopped, or 6–8 cherry tomatoes, halved

2 spring onions, thinly sliced

Dressing

3 tbsp light olive oil

1 tbsp runny honey

1 tbsp soy sauce

1 tbsp fresh lemon juice

Step one Cook the pasta in lightly salted boiling water according to the instructions on the packet. Steam the broccoli florets for 5 minutes. Meanwhile, whisk together all the ingredients for the dressing.

Step two Put the chopped turkey or chicken, sweetcorn, tomatoes and spring onions into a bowl together with the drained pasta and toss with the dressing.

Caramelised red onion and mozzarella wraps

Warm caramelised red onions with balsamic vinegar and mozzarella make a delicious filling for a wrap. You can prepare the onions in advance and then simply re-heat when ready to assemble.

Step one Heat the oil in a non-stick frying pan, add the onions and thyme and stir over a low heat for 15 minutes. Stir in the sugar, balsamic vinegar and seasoning and continue to cook for 5 minutes. Turn the heat up and cook for 1 minute until all the liquid has evaporated. Remove from the heat and allow to cool.

Step two Heat the tortillas according to the packet instructions – either in a microwave or in a dry frying pan. Divide the cooked onion mixture between the tortillas, slice the mozzarella and lay on top of the onions and season. Toss the rocket leaves with the oil and balsamic vinegar and place on top of the mozzarella cheese. Roll up the tortillas and then cut in half diagonally before serving.

Serves 2

1 tbsp olive oil

2 medium red onions, peeled and thinly sliced

1½ tsp fresh thyme, chopped

2 tsp brown sugar

2 tsp balsamic vinegar

2 tortillas

125g (4½ oz) ball mozzarella

20g (¾ oz) rocket leaves (about a handful)

¼ tsp olive oil

few drops balsamic vinegar

salt and freshly ground black pepper

Tuna melt

Try this nutritious, tasty, quick and easy snack. If you wish you can use half-fat crème fraîche and Cheddar. This is also good for breakfast.

Serves 2

1 x 200g (7oz) tin tuna in brine

2 tbsp tomato ketchup

2 tbsp crème fraîche

1 or 2 finely sliced spring onions (optional)

2 English muffins

40g (1½oz) Cheddar, grated

Step one Drain the brine from the tuna and flake into small pieces. Mix together with the tomato ketchup, crème fraîche and spring onions (if using).

Step two Split the muffins and toast them. Spread with the tuna mixture and sprinkle with the grated Cheddar. Place the muffins under a preheated grill until the cheese is golden and bubbling.

Bagel snake

This is a fun way of arranging sandwiches and I find that bagels are popular with both children and their mums and dads. You can make the snake as long as you like, depending on how many bagels you use and you can use a variety of toppings. I have chosen tuna and egg toppings, which are both nutritious, but, of course, there is an infinite variety of ingredients that you could choose, such as cream cheese and cucumber.

Step one Slice the bagels in half and then cut each half down the centre to form a semi-circle. Cut out the head of the snake from one of the pieces of bagel and the tail from another. Mix the ingredients for the tuna topping and mix the ingredients for the egg topping. Spread half the bagels with tuna and half with egg.

Step two Decorate the tuna topping with halved cherry tomatoes and the egg topping with strips of chives arranged in a criss-cross pattern. Arrange the bagels to form the body of a snake. Then attach the head to the snake's body and arrange two slices of stuffed olive to form the eyes and cut out a forked tongue from the strip of red pepper.

Serves 2

2 bagels

Tuna and cheese topping

1 x 200g (7oz) tin of tuna in sunflower oil (drained)

2 tbsp tomato ketchup

2 tbsp crème fraîche

2 spring onions, finely sliced

Egg mayonnaise with salad cress

2 or 3 hard-boiled eggs (10 minutes)

45ml (3 tbsp) mayonnaise

1 tbsp chives

3 tbsp salad cress

salt and freshly ground black pepper

Decoration

cherry tomatoes, halved

chives

1 stuffed olive, sliced

strip of red pepper

Little Gem cups

Instead of making sandwiches, why not use the boat-shaped leaves of Little Gem lettuces to hold delicious fillings?

Makes 4 or 6 Little Gem cups each type

Chicken and mango Little Gems

75g (3oz) cooked chicken breast, shredded

75g (3oz) chopped ripe mango

½ spring onion, finely sliced

1 tbsp lemon juice and 1 tsp lemon zest

2 tsp honey

1½ tbsp light olive

6 Little Gem lettuce leaves

Prawn and watercress Little Gems

100g (3½ oz) small cooked prawns

2 tbsp light mayonnaise

1 tbsp tomato ketchup

handful of watercress, trimmed and chopped

a little paprika

4 Little Gem lettuce leaves

Step one Mix the ingredients together, except the lettuce, for either recipe. Spoon some of the mixture into each lettuce leaf and sprinkle the prawn mixture with paprika.

Tasty vegetable wrap

A delicious combination of caramelised onion, sweet pepper, tomatoes and grated cheese.

Step one Heat the oil in a frying pan. Add the onions and gently fry until soft, then add the balsamic vinegar and sugar. Throw in the yellow pepper and fry with the onions for 5 minutes. Add the thyme and tomatoes and season to taste.

Step two Warm the tortillas in the microwave. Put some of the mixture in the middle of the wrap. Sprinkle over the Cheddar and rocket. Roll up tightly. Repeat with the remaining wraps.

Makes 4 wraps

1 tbsp olive oil

2 small red onions, sliced

1 tsp balsamic vinegar

a pinch of sugar

1 yellow pepper, deseeded and thinly sliced

1 tbsp fresh thyme, chopped

2 tomatoes, deseeded and roughly chopped or 110g 4oz) cherry tomatoes, quartered

60g (2¼ oz) Cheddar, grated

60g (2oz) rocket

4 tortilla wraps

Baked parsnip and sweet potato crisps

Kids who don't always like vegetables may be fooled into eating these crisps as they are naturally slightly sweet and very delicious. And they are healthier too, as they are baked rather than fried. Not suitable for freezing or reheating.

Serves 4

1 small parsnip, peeled

½ small sweet potato, peeled

1 tbsp olive oil

pinch of salt (optional)

Step one Preheat the oven to 150°C/300°F/gas 2 and line two large baking sheets with non-stick baking parchment.

Step two Use a small swivel peeler to peel thin strips from the parsnip. Put the strips in a bowl and toss with half of the oil. Spread out in a single layer on one of the prepared baking sheets. Do the same with the sweet potato, spreading the strips on the second baking sheet.

Step three Bake for 10 minutes then swap the baking sheets around. Bake for a further 5 minutes then check and remove from the oven if the crisps are crisp and browned at the edges. Otherwise continue cooking for a further 4–5 minutes, checking every minute, as the crisps can go brown very quickly. You may find that the parsnips cook slightly more quickly than the potato (see Tip below).

Step four Transfer the cooked crisps to a bowl and sprinkle over a pinch of salt, if you like. These are best served the day they are made but can be stored in an airtight container overnight (they may soften a bit).

The potato and parsnip cook at slightly different rates so it is easier to cook them on separate baking sheets. Watch them carefully towards the end of the cooking time.

Coconut shrimp

Coconut shrimp is a hugely popular dish in America. I'm not sure who thought of the addition of coconut originally, but the flavour seems to complement the sweetness of the prawns. I love the very light and crispy Japanese panko breadcrumbs, but if you can't find them then use ordinary dried breadcrumbs instead. Not suitable for freezing or reheating.

Step one Mix the dipping sauce ingredients together in a small bowl. Divide among four smaller dipping bowls and set aside.

Step two Pat the prawns dry with kitchen paper. Spread the flour out on a large plate. Whisk the egg and soy sauce together in a bowl. Mix the breadcrumbs and coconut together and spread out on a second plate. Dust the prawns with flour then dip in the egg and roll in the coconut breadcrumbs. Transfer to a plate or tray. The breadcrumb-coated prawns can be kept in the fridge, covered, for 2 hours before cooking.

Step three Put some sunflower oil in a wok or deep-sided frying pan, to the depth of 1 cm (½ in). Heat over a medium heat, until a breadcrumb dropped into the oil sizzles and browns in around 30 seconds. Add the coated prawns and cook for 2–3 minutes each side, until golden. If the prawns are browning too quickly then lower the heat slightly. Don't overcrowd the pan – you may need to cook the prawns in two batches. Drain the cooked prawns on a couple of layers of kitchen paper and allow to cool slightly, then serve with dipping sauce.

Serves 3–4 (recipe easily halved or doubled)

Dipping sauce

2 tbsp sweet chilli sauce

2 tsp rice wine vinegar

1 tsp mirin

13 raw tiger prawns (defrosted if frozen), peeled and de-veined

2 tbsp flour

1 egg

½ tsp dark soy sauce

30g (1oz) panko or dried breadcrumbs

20g (¾oz) desiccated coconut

sunflower oil, for frying

Annabel's chicken rissoles

You can sneak some vegetables into these tasty chicken rissoles. It is good to make a batch and freeze them on a baking tray lined with clingfilm.

Makes 12 rissoles

175g (6oz) white breadcrumbs, crusts removed

1½ tbsp milk

150g (5¼ oz) carrots, grated

150g (5¼ oz) courgette, grated

2 tbsp sunflower oil, for frying

150g (5¼ oz) onion, finely chopped

1 garlic clove, crushed

200g (7oz) minced chicken

1 tsp dried oregano

1 tbsp tomato ketchup

½ tbsp maple syrup

1 tsp soy sauce

½ tsp Worcestershire sauce

½ tsp balsamic vinegar

½ tsp caster sugar

salt and freshly ground black pepper,

Coating

30g (1oz) flour

1 egg, beaten

3½ tbsp oil, for frying

salt and freshly ground black pepper

Step one Put 75g (3oz) of the breadcrumbs into a bowl then add the milk and leave to soak for 10 minutes. Squeeze a little of the moisture from the grated carrot and courgette.

Step two Heat the sunflower oil in a frying pan and sauté the onion for 3 minutes, stirring occasionally. Add the garlic and cook for 30 seconds, then add the carrot and courgette, stirring for 5 minutes over a low heat. Transfer to a plate and keep cool.

Step three Mix together the bread soaked in milk, the chicken, cooked veg and remaining ingredients, and season with a little salt and pepper.

Step four To coat the rissoles, spread out the flour on a large plate. Beat the egg in a small bowl. Using floured hands, form the mixture into rissoles, coat in the flour, dip in the egg and then coat with the remaining breadcrumbs. Heat the oil in the frying pan and fry the rissoles for 12 minutes, turning occasionally, until golden brown.

American–Italian mini meatballs

You can substitute chicken mince for veal or pork, or use just one type of mince. Cooked meatballs can be frozen (see tip below).

Step one Preheat the oven to 200°C/400°F/gas 6 if using the oven method. Put a lipped baking sheet in the oven.

Step two First, make the sauce. Heat the oil in a large pan and sauté the onion for 10 minutes, until soft. Add the garlic, cook for 1 minute, then transfer half to a food processor. Add the tomatoes, purées, sugar, oregano and vegetable stock to the onion in the pan, bring to a boil, reduce the heat and simmer for 25 minutes.

Step three Meanwhile, add the beef, veal and pork mince to the onion in the food-processor. Whizz for a minute to chop everything up, then add the breadcrumbs, milk, parsley, Parmesan and salt and pepper to taste. Pulse until well combined. Take rounded teaspoonfuls of the meatball mixture and form them into about 30 small balls. You can now either fry the meatballs or cook them in the oven.

Step four For frying, heat the oil in a large non-stick frying pan and fry in batches of 8–10 meatballs for 2–3 minutes on each side, until golden. Drain on kitchen paper. For oven browning, put 2 tablespoons of sunflower oil on the hot baking sheet and add the meatballs. Bake for 20 minutes, turning halfway through.

Step five Purée the tomato sauce until smooth, and season to taste with salt and pepper. Return to the pan and add the drained browned meatballs. Simmer for a further 5–10 minutes. Serve with spaghetti or in hollowed-out French bread.

The meatballs are suitable for reheating: brown the meatballs, allow to cool, then mix them with the cooled sauce. Reheat gently in a pan for 10–15 minutes or bake for 25 minutes in a preheated oven at 200°C/400°F/gas 6, until piping hot.

Serves 8–12

Sauce

1 tbsp olive oil

1 medium red onion, chopped

1 garlic clove, crushed

1 x 400g (14oz) tin chopped tomatoes

1½ tbsp tomato purée

1 tbsp sun-dried tomato purée

1 tsp soft light brown sugar

¼ tsp dried oregano

50ml (2fl oz) vegetable stock

110g (4oz) beef mince

110g (4oz) veal mince

110g (4oz) pork mince

30g (1oz) fresh white breadcrumbs

3 tbsp milk

small handful of parsley leaves, chopped

2 tbsp freshly grated Parmesan

2–3 tbsp sunflower oil, for frying

salt and freshly ground black pepper

Minty lamb koftas

Children love to eat things on sticks, and sometimes I have called these 'lamb lollies' to increase the appeal. However, the koftas are also good stuffed into pittas or wraps (remove the skewer first) or even for making into slightly larger lamb burgers. Not suitable for freezing.

Makes 8 koftas

1 small red onion, finely chopped

1 tbsp olive oil

1 garlic clove, crushed

½ tsp ground cumin

225 (8oz) minced lamb

20g (¾oz) fresh breadcrumbs from 1 slice of bread, crusts removed

2 tsp chopped fresh mint leaves

1 tsp clear honey

1 egg yolk

salt and freshly ground black pepper

Step one Soak 8 wooden skewers in warm water for 30 or so minutes. Sauté the onion in the oil for 5–6 minutes, until soft. Add the garlic and cumin, and cook for an extra minute, then transfer to a bowl. Add the remaining ingredients, season to taste with salt and pepper, and mix thoroughly. For a finer texture pulse everything in a food processor.

Step two Divide the mixture into 8 and form into balls. Thread a skewer through each ball and use your hand firmly to form each ball into a sausage shape on the skewer. If possible chill the koftas for 1–2 hours.

Step three Preheat the grill to high. Grill the koftas for 8–10 minutes, turning halfway, until cooked through. Cool slightly before serving and remove the skewers for smaller children.

Leftovers will keep for up to 2 days in the fridge and so are suitable for reheating (skewers removed). Reheat in a microwave for 20–30 seconds per kofta; otherwise wrap meat in foil and bake at 180°C/350°F/gas 4 for 15 minutes, or until piping hot.

Grandma's noodle pudding

These are a tasty snack, particularly to satisfy your sweet tooth cravings mid-afternoon.

Step one Preheat the oven to 180°C/350°F/gas 4.

Step two Cook the vermicelli or fine egg noodles in boiling salted water for about 5 minutes. Drain. Mix with the remaining ingredients, apart from the knob of butter.

Step three Tip the mixture into a 25 x 20cm (10 x 8in) greased ovenproof dish. Dot with butter and bake for 40 minutes.

Serves 6

225g (8oz) vermicelli or fine egg noodles

1 large egg, beaten

25g (1oz) butter, melted, plus a knob for the topping

100ml (0½ fl oz) milk

2 tbsp vanilla sugar or 2 tbsp caster sugar and 1 tsp vanilla essence

½ tsp mixed spice

100g (3½oz) each sultanas and raisins

15g (½oz) flaked almonds (optional)

Trail mix bars

Trail mix is a snack food commonly used in outdoor recreational activities such as hiking, backpacking and mountaineering. It usually consists of a mixture of nuts, seeds and dried fruits such as raisins and cranberries. It's energy rich and has a high content of vitamins and minerals. .

Serves 8

55g (2oz) butter

3 tbsp golden syrup or clear honey

100g (3½ oz) quick-cook oats

80g (3oz) soft brown sugar

30g (1oz) Cheerios

40g (1½ oz) raisins

40g (1½ oz) salted peanuts or pumpkin seeds

55g (2oz) milk chocolate chips or dried cranberries

35g (1¼ oz) sunflower seeds

¼ tsp salt

Step one Preheat the oven to 170°C/325°F/gas 3 and line a 20 x 20cm (8 x 8in) tin with greased baking parchment.

Step two Put the butter and golden syrup in a small pan over a low heat until the butter has melted. Set aside to cool.

Step three Put the remaining ingredients in a large bowl and stir together. Add the cooled butter mixture and mix well to combine. Transfer the mixture to the prepared tin and press down firmly. Bake for 30–35 minutes until the centre is just firm to the touch.

Step four Remove from the oven, cool for 15 minutes then mark into 8 bars, using a sharp knife. Allow to cool completely before lifting from the pan. Store in an airtight container.

Cranberry jelly with summer berries

It's easy to make your own jelly from fruit juice. Leaf gelatine is amazing. It dissolves like a dream every time. You should be able to buy it in large supermarkets. Alternatively you could use powdered gelatine. By setting the jelly in two layers, you will get the berries set in the jelly on top and the clear jelly underneath. I used individual plastic 150ml (¼ pint) jelly moulds, which have detachable tops – this helps to release the jelly when set. You could, however, use one large jelly mould or simply set the jelly in glass bowls

Step one To make the jelly, place the leaf gelatine in a shallow dish and pour over just enough cranberry and raspberry juice to cover. Leave to soften for about 5 minutes.

Step two Heat half the remaining cranberry and raspberry juice with the caster sugar in a saucepan until bubbling. Mix in the softened leaf gelatine and any remaining juice, stirring until completely dissolved. Set aside to cool down a little, then stir in the rest of the cranberry and raspberry juice. (If you are using powdered gelatine, you will need to put 6 tablespoons of the cranberry and raspberry juice in a small saucepan, sprinkle the gelatine over, then leave to stand for 5 minutes. Put the pan over a low heat and let the gelatine dissolve. Stir gently but do not allow to boil. Put a quarter of the remaining juice and the sugar into a small pan and stir over a medium heat until dissolved, then mix together with the remaining cranberry and raspberry juice and the dissolved gelatine.)

Step three Divide the berries between 6 individual jelly moulds (or use 4 x 175ml individual pudding basins) and pour over the juice until the berries are just covered. (Alternatively, you could set the jelly in one large 750ml/1½ pint jelly mould or glass bowl.) It's a good idea to rinse the moulds first and leave a little water clinging to the sides – this can help stop the jelly from sticking. Leave in the fridge until set.

Serves 6

8 gelatine leaves (approx 12g) or 1¼ x 11g sachets powdered gelatine

600ml (1 pint) cranberry and raspberry juice drink or cranberry juice

40g (1½ oz) caster sugar

175g (6oz) mixed berries (raspberries, blueberries and strawberries (quartered)

Raspberry ripple cheesecake

This is a fabulously easy cheesecake, but do use the cream cheese at room temperature, or the gelatine will harden quickly and go lumpy.

Serves 8

7 gelatine leaves (approx. 12g) or 1 x 11g sachet powdered gelatine

100g (3½ oz) butter

200g (7oz) digestive biscuits, crushed with a rolling pin

150g (5¼ oz) fresh raspberries

2 tbsp icing sugar

1 tbsp cornflour

450g (1lb) cream cheese, at room temperature

225g (8oz) caster sugar

2 tsp vanilla extract

400ml (12fl oz) double cream

300g (10½ oz) fresh berries for topping, e.g. raspberries, strawberries, blackberries

85g (3½ oz) white chocolate

Step one If using gelatine leaves, soak them in 150ml (5fl oz) water for 5 minutes, then remove, squeezing out excess water, and place in a bowl over a pan of simmering water for about 30 seconds, stirring until melted. Set aside to cool. If using powdered gelatine, put 3 tablespoons water into a small saucepan, sprinkle over the gelatine and leave to stand for 5 minutes. Put the pan over a low heat and stir gently for 1 minute until the gelatine has dissolved. Set aside to cool.

Step two Melt the butter in a large pan and stir in the crushed biscuits. Spread the mixture over the base of a 20cm (8in) round cake tin, pressing it down, then place in the fridge.

Step three Blitz the raspberries together with the icing sugar in a food processor, then press through a sieve into a small pan to get rid of any seeds. Remove 1 tablespoon of the raspberry coulis and mix with the cornflour. Stir this into the raspberry coulis in the pan, bring to the boil, then allow to cool.

Step four Beat together the cream cheese, sugar and vanilla until smooth. Remove 6 tablespoons and stir into the gelatine. Beat the cream until stiff. Fold the cream into the cream cheese mixture, together with the cream cheese and gelatine mixture.

Step five Remove the cake tin from the fridge and spread half the cheesecake mixture over the base. Spoon half the raspberry coulis in blobs onto the cheesecake mix, then, using a skewer, swirl it through to make a ripple effect. Spoon the remaining cheesecake mixture on top and level the surface with a palette knife. Decorate the top of the cake by trailing lines of raspberry coulis from a teaspoon. Use a skewer to draw vertical lines through the coulis to create a pattern. Place in the fridge to set. Once set, arrange the berries on top. Melt the chocolate in a heatproof bowl over a pan of simmering water, then pour into a piping bag and pipe zig-zag lines of chocolate over the fruit.

The perfect lemon polenta cake

It can be hard to find a truly delicious cake that doesn't contain any flour. Yes, you can buy gluten-free cakes but sadly I often find them disappointing, so I rang Ruth Rogers and Rose Gray of the River Café to see if I could include their wonderful polenta cake in my books – this recipe comes from the original *River Café Cookbook*. I am sure many children, regardless of whether they suffer a wheat allergy or not, will be very grateful.

Step one Preheat the oven to 160°C/325°F/gas 3. Butter and flour a 30cm (12in) cake tin.

Step two Using an electric mixer, beat the butter and sugar together until pale and light. Stir in the ground almonds and vanilla. Beat in the eggs, one at a time. Fold in the lemon zest and juice, polenta, baking powder and salt.

Step three Spoon the mixture into the prepared tin and bake for 45–50 minutes or until set. The cake will be brown on top. Serve on its own or with ice cream.

Serves 10

450g (1lb) unsalted butter, softened

450g (1lb) caster sugar

450g (1lb) almonds, ground

2 tsp vanilla extract

6 eggs

grated zest of 4 lemons

juice of 1 lemon

225g (8oz) polenta

1 tsp baking powder

¼ tsp salt

gluten-free flour for dusting

Lara's favourite brownies

My daughter Lara adores chocolate. She loves to make these brownies and share them with her friends. Good news for teenagers; the idea that chocolate can cause acne is not supported by any scientific evidence. These are good served warm with vanilla ice cream and hot chocolate sauce (see tip below).

Makes 8 brownies

175g (6oz) unsalted butter

125g (4½ oz) good-quality plain chocolate, broken into pieces

3 large eggs

150g (5¼ oz) golden caster sugar

75g (3oz) ground almonds

75g (3oz) plain flour

50g (2oz) plain chocolate chips

50g (2oz) white chocolate, broken into pieces

icing sugar, sifted, to dust

Step one Preheat the oven to 180°C/350°F/gas 4. Grease and line a 20cm (8in) square cake tin.

Step two Cut the butter into pieces, put them in a heatproof bowl with the plain chocolate and place over a pan of simmering water. Stir until melted.

Step three Whisk the eggs and sugar together with an electric mixer for about 5 minutes or until thickened and fluffy. Stir in the melted chocolate mixture. Fold in the ground almonds, flour, plain chocolate chips and white chocolate chunks. Pour the mixture into the tin. Bake for about 25 minutes or until well risen and slightly firm at the edges. The brownie will still be soft in the centre. Leave to cool in the tin, then turn out and dust the top with sifted icing sugar. Cut into squares before serving.

To make a quick chocolate sauce melt 110g (4oz) plain chocolate with 1 tablespoon of golden syrup. Cool slightly and stir in 150ml (¼ pint) single cream.

For more recipes from My Kitchen Table, sign up for our newsletter at www.mykitchentable.co.uk/newsletter

KITCHEN TABLE

Chocolate fridge cake

These chocolate biscuit squares are a particular favourite of mine. You can also experiment with other combinations of biscuits, fruit and nuts; for example, you could make this using half digestive and half ginger biscuits and with dried cranberries instead of the raisins. This will keep for up to 2 weeks in the fridge. Well, maybe not!

Step one Line the tin with clingfilm, leaving enough to hang over the sides of a 20cm (8in) square, shallow cake tin.

Step two Break the biscuits into small pieces. Melt the two chocolates, syrup and butter in a heatproof bowl over a pan of simmering water, stirring occasionally. Make sure that the bottom of the bowl doesn't touch the water.

Step three Mix together the biscuits, apricots, raisins, pecans and Rice Krispies. Stir these into the melted chocolate mixture. Spoon the mixture into the prepared tin and level the surface by pressing down with a potato masher. Leave to cool in the tin then place in the fridge to set (which will take 1–2 hours). To serve, turn out, carefully peel off the cling film and cut into 12 squares.

Serves 12

150g (5oz) digestive biscuits

100g (3½oz) milk chocolate

100g (3½oz) plain chocolate

100g (3½oz) golden syrup

75g (3oz) unsalted butter

75g (3oz) dried apricots, chopped

50g (2oz) raisins

50g (2oz) pecans, finely chopped

25g (1oz) Rice Krispies

Chocolate puddings with chocolate fudge sauce

This is always a favourite in my house. Even the fussiest of eaters wouldn't say no to this! Suitable for freezing.

Serves 8

Chocolate sponge

125g (4½ oz) butter, at room temperature, plus 1 tbsp extra for greasing

125g (4½ oz) soft light brown sugar

3 large eggs, lightly beaten

100g (3½ oz) plain flour

25g (1oz) cocoa powder

2 tsp baking powder

¼ tsp salt

75g (2½ oz) plain chocolate, chopped

Chocolate fudge sauce

100g (3½ oz) plain chocolate, chopped

4 tbsp soft light brown sugar

2 tbsp golden syrup

20g (¾oz) butter

200ml (7fl oz) double cream

vanilla ice cream, to serve

Step one Preheat the oven to 180°C/350°F/gas 4. Grease 8 small pudding basins and line bases with circles of baking parchment.

Step two Cream the butter and sugar until fluffy. Add the eggs and sift over the flour, cocoa, baking powder and salt and beat until just combined. Fold in the chocolate.

Step three Spoon the batter into the prepared basins (to half full). Bake for 20 minutes until risen and firm to the touch. Allow to cool slightly, then turn out the puddings (you may need to run a knife around the edge).

Step four To make the fudge sauce, put all of the ingredients in a medium pan and heat gently until smooth. Bring to a boil then remove from the heat and pour over the warm puddings. Serve with vanilla ice cream.

You could also bake the chocolate sponge in a 20 x 20cm (8 x 8in) cake tin lined with parchment. Baking time may be a bit longer (30–35 minutes). Cut into squares and serve with the chocolate sauce.

Elderflower jelly

You could use a mixture of berry fruits instead of the peaches, pear and grapes. If you have never used leaf gelatine, you will be surprised how it dissolves perfectly every time, so now making jelly is really easy. You can buy leaf gelatine in most supermarkets.

Step one Mix the cordial with the cold water in a jug. Soak the gelatine for 5 minutes in just enough cold water to cover. Meanwhile, warm 100ml (3fl oz) of the cordial mix in a medium pan until hot but not boiling. Remove from the heat.

Step two Squeeze out any excess water from the gelatine. Stir the gelatine into the warm cordial until fully dissolved. Add the remaining cordial mix and the lemon juice, and stir well. You must add the remaining cordial to the dissolved gelatine and not vice versa, or it can cause the gelatine to go stringy.

Step three Divide the fruit among four small glasses and pour in the cordial mix. Chill overnight.

Serves 4

300ml (10½ fl oz) elderflower cordial

400ml (14fl oz) cold water

6 gelatine leaves

1 tsp fresh lemon juice

125g (4½ oz) mixed fruit, e.g. chopped peaches (tinned or fresh), a tin of fruit cocktail, or a mixture of berry fruits

Strawberry and rhubarb crumble

This is one of my favourite crumbles. It is a delicious combination of flavours and the pink colour of the rhubarb looks so attractive. It is also very quick and easy to prepare. Serve with custard or ice cream.

Serves 5

Crumble topping

150g (5¼ oz) plain flour

pinch of salt

100g (3½ oz) cold butter, cut into pieces

75g (3oz) demerara sugar

50g (2oz) ground almonds

400g (14oz) rhubarb

100g (3½ oz) strawberries

4 tbsp caster sugar

25g (1oz) ground almonds

Step one Preheat the oven to 200°C/400°F/gas 6.

Step two To make the topping, mix the flour together with a generous pinch of salt in a bowl and rub in the butter using your fingertips until the mixture resembles breadcrumbs. Then rub in the demerara sugar and ground almonds.

Step three Cut the rhubarb into small pieces and halve the strawberries. Sprinkle the ground almonds over the base of a suitable ovenproof dish (a round pyrex dish with a 17cm/7in diameter is good). Mix the rhubarb and strawberries together with the sugar, and spoon into the dish.

Step four Cover the fruit with the crumble topping and sprinkle over a tablespoon of water, which will help to make the topping crispy. Bake in the oven until the topping becomes golden brown (about 25 minutes).

Frozen berries with hot white chocolate sauce

This is served up in some of the poshest restaurants as dessert, but it's dead simple to make at home and oh so plate-lickingly good that I defy the fussiest eater to refuse it! It's best to freeze the berries yourself (see tip below), as ready-frozen berries tend to go a bit mushy when defrosted. This is a particular favourite of my daughter Lara, who has always been a bit fussy.

Step one Take the berries out of the freezer and divide between two bowls. Allow them to defrost slightly at room temperature for around 10 minutes.

Step two Put the chocolate and cream in a microwaveable jug and cook for 10 seconds, stir and repeat heating and stirring until chocolate has just melted (it will take 4–5 blasts) and you have a smooth sauce. Alternatively, put the cream and chocolate in a small bowl over a pan of simmering water and stir continuously until the chocolate has just melted

Step three Pour the hot sauce immediately over the berries and serve at once.

To freeze the berries, line a rimmed baking sheet with parchment or greaseproof paper and arrange the berries in a single layer. When they are frozen, transfer to small freezer bags. They will last for 1 month and are also good in smoothies

Serves 2

150g (5½ oz) frozen mixed berries (e.g. blackberries, raspberries, blueberries, strawberries, redcurrants)

55g (2oz) white chocolate, chopped into small pieces

4 tbsp double cream

Frozen yoghurts

I adore frozen yoghurt and it is less rich than ice cream. Lychee is one of my favourite flavours and is very refreshing. It's worth investing in an ice cream maker – once you've tasted this you'll want to make it again and again. You can also make frozen yoghurt using frozen fruits.

Luscious lychee frozen yoghurt

Serves 6

500ml (17½ fl oz) full-fat natural yoghurt (500g/1lb 2oz pot)

150ml (¼ pint) single cream

75g (3oz) caster sugar

425g (15oz) tin lychees

Step one Mix together the yoghurt, cream and sugar. Blend the lychees together with 200ml (7fl oz) of the juice from the tin. Freeze and churn the mixture in an ice cream maker. If you don't have an ice cream maker, pour the mixture into a shallow container, place in the freezer for 1 hour, then transfer to a food processor and whiz until smooth. Freeze for 2 hours, then process again before freezing until firm.

Summer berry yoghurt ice

Serves 6

200g (7oz) mixed frozen summer fruits; (e.g. strawberries, raspberries, blackberries, blueberries, cherries or redcurrants)

75g (3oz) and 1 tbsp caster sugar

200ml (7fl oz) double cream

400ml (14fl oz) mild natural yoghurt (e.g. Onken set yoghurt)

Step one Put the frozen berries in a small saucepan together with 1 tablespoon of the caster sugar and cook over a gentle heat for a few minutes until soft. Purée the fruit and press through a sieve to get rid of the seeds.

Step two Whip the cream until it forms soft peaks. Mix together the cream, yoghurt, the rest of the sugar and the fruit purée. Freeze in an ice cream maker or spoon into a suitable container and put in the freezer. When half-frozen (about an hour) beat it well until smooth. Return to the freezer and stir one or two more times during the remaining hour of freezing to get a smooth ice cream.

Lollies

If there is one food that almost no child can resist it has to be an ice lolly. It's easy to make your own by puréeing fruits and mixing the purée with fruit juice or yoghurt. You could also simply freeze pure fruit juice or fruit smoothies in ice-lolly moulds. Most manufactured lollies are full of artificial flavouring and colouring so why not make your own? Strawberries contain higher levels of vitamin C than any other berry.

Watermelon cooler

Step one Blitz the watermelon together with the icing sugar and pour into lolly moulds. Freeze for 2–3 hours or until solid.

Makes 6 small lollies

300g (10oz) watermelon, deseeded and cubed

75g (3oz) icing sugar

Strawberry sorbet ice lollies

Step one Put the sugar and 40ml (2fl oz) of water in a saucepan and boil until syrupy (about 3 minutes). Allow to cool.

Step two Purée the strawberries with an electric hand blender and combine with the cooled syrup and orange juice, then pour this mixture into the ice lolly moulds. Freeze until solid.

30g (1¾oz) caster sugar

250g (9oz) strawberries, hulled and cut in half

juice of 1 medium orange (approx. 40ml/2fl oz)

Tropical lollies

Step one Blend the ingredients together until smooth. Pour into 4 large ice-lolly moulds and freeze.

1 large mango, stoned peeled and diced

180ml (6fl oz) tropical fruit juice

3 tbsp icing sugar

1 tbsp fresh lemon juice

Cranberry and white chocolate cookies

These are not to be missed: probably my favourite cookies and so quick and easy to make. You can buy dried cranberries in the supermarket.

Makes 20 cookies

150g (5¼ oz) plain flour

½ tsp bicarbonate of soda

½ tsp salt

25g (1oz) ground almonds

150g (5¼ oz) soft brown sugar

50g (2oz) porridge oats

50g (2oz) dried cranberries

40g (1½ oz) white chocolate, cut into chunks

150g (5¼ oz) butter

1 large egg yolk or 2 small egg yolks

Step one Preheat the oven to 190°C/375°F/gas 5.

Step two Sieve together the flour, bicarbonate of soda and salt in a large bowl. Stir in the ground almonds, brown sugar, porridge oats, cranberries and white chocolate chunks.

Step three Melt the butter in a small pan. Stir this into the dry ingredients together with the egg yolk. Mix well, then using your hands, form into walnut-sized balls and arrange on two large non-stick baking sheets. Gently press them down to flatten slightly, leaving space between them for the biscuits to spread. Bake in the oven for 12 minutes, then remove and allow to cool on a wire rack.

Strawberry cream cake

A simple and quick cake to make – and it's sure to be a great favourite with everyone in the family.

Step one Preheat the oven to 180°C/350°F/gas 4 and line and grease two 20cm (8in) sandwich tins.

Step two Beat together the margarine and sugar, then add the eggs, one at a time, adding 1 tablespoon of flour with the eggs after the first egg to stop the mixture from curdling. Beat in the remaining flour, the lemon zest, vanilla essence and water until light and fluffy.

Step three Divide the mixture between the prepared sandwich tins and bake in the oven for about 20 minutes or until lightly golden and risen. Turn them out of the tins and put on a wire rack to cool.

Step four To make the filling/topping, whip the cream with the icing sugar until firm. Thinly slice 100g (4oz) of the strawberries. Stir the strawberries into two thirds of the whipping cream. Spread the strawberry jam over one of the cakes, top with the strawberries and cream mixture and place the other cake on top. Using the remaining cream, pipe rosettes around the cake and place half a strawberry on top of each rosette. Keep refrigerated until ready to serve.

Serves 8

175g (6oz) soft margarine

175g (6oz) soft brown sugar

3 large eggs, beaten

175g (6oz) self raising flour

½ tsp lemon zest

1 tsp vanilla essence

1 tbsp water

Filling/topping

300ml (½ pint) whipping or double cream

3 tbsp icing sugar

150g (5¼ oz) strawberries

2–3 tbsp strawberry jam

Berried treasure

You can buy rose water in many supermarkets and it gives this fruit compote a lovely flavour. The pomegranate seeds add a crunchy texture that complements the berry fruits.

Serves 4

2 peaches

20g (½oz) butter

2 tbsp golden caster sugar

1 tbsp rose water

100g (3½oz) strawberries

100g (3½oz) blackberries

100g (3½oz) blueberries

100g (3½oz) raspberries

½ pomegranate (optional)

Step one Halve and stone the peaches, and cut each half into four slices. Melt the butter in a heavy-bottomed saucepan and sauté the peaches for 1 minute. Sprinkle with the sugar and cook for 1 minute more. Add the rose water and the strawberries, blackberries and blueberries, and heat for about 1 minute. Remove from the heat and stir in the raspberries and pomegranate seeds.

Fruit flowers

Some fun ways to get your five a day! The pineapple-melon flowers would make a great centrepiece on a table.

Kiwi–raspberry flowers

Step one Peel the kiwi fruits and cut 4 round slices approximately 1.5cm (½in) thick from the centre section of each kiwi fruit (leftover kiwi fruit can be cubed and used in a fruit salad). Cut each slice into a flower shape using the cookie cutter. Arrange the kiwi flowers on a plate and top each one with a raspberry.

2 large firm kiwi fruits

8 raspberries

Chocolate-dipped strawberry 'buds'

Step one Put the chocolate in a heatproof bowl and melt it over a pan of warm water, stirring occasionally. Insert the tip of a skewer into a strawberry and hold the fruit over the bowl. Spoon melted chocolate over the strawberry, turning it so it is completely coated. Allow excess chocolate to drip off, then stand the skewer in a glass in a cool place to let the chocolate set.

Step two If you like, you could pipe swirls or squiggles in contrasting melted chocolate over the strawberries.

100g (3½ oz) white, plain or milk chocolate (according to your preference), chopped into pieces

8 strawberries, hulled

Pineapple–melon flowers

Step one Cut the pineapple into round slices around 1cm (generous ¼in) thick. Use a 7cm (3in) flower-shaped cookie cutter to cut one flower from each slice. It may be easier to press the cutter into the pineapple then cut around the shape with a small sharp knife. Use a round cookie cutter (2.5cm/1in diameter) to cut a hole in the centre of each flower.

Step two Pat the pineapple flowers with kitchen towel to remove excess juice. Carve 12 balls of melon with a melon baller the same diameter as the round cookie cutter. Make the flower centre by pushing a melon ball through the hole cut in each pineapple piece. Thread each flower onto a skewer (going through the pineapple and the melon) to secure. Cover the skewer with a green straw.

1 large ripe pineapple, all skin removed

1 cantaloupe melon, halved and deseeded

Ginger snaps

Children are very fond of crisp ginger biscuits, and these little ginger snaps fit the bill perfectly. Dipping the teaspoon in water when scooping the dough will help to give you beautifully round biscuits. These are extremely yummy and so easy to prepare. The cooked and cooled biscuits can be frozen for up to 1 month.

Makes approx. 28 ginger snaps

50g (2oz) butter, softened

100g (3½ oz) soft light brown sugar

1 egg yolk

2 tbsp golden syrup

100g (3½ oz) plain flour

2 tsp ground ginger

¼ tsp bicarbonate of soda

pinch of salt (optional)

Step one Preheat the oven to 150°C/300°F/gas 2. Line a baking sheet with non-stick baking parchment.

Step two Beat the butter, sugar, egg and syrup together in a large bowl until fluffy and slightly paler in colour.

Step three Sift over the dry ingredients and mix to form a soft dough. Dip a round measuring teaspoon in a glass of water and scoop up a slightly rounded teaspoon of the dough, then drop it on to a baking sheet. Continue dipping the teaspoon and scooping the remaining dough, leaving 5–6 cm (about 2 in) between each mound of dough as the biscuits will spread. You may need to bake the biscuits in batches. Bake the biscuits for 14–16 minutes, until light brown around the edges. Remove from the oven and leave to cool for 5 minutes, then use a palette knife or fish slice to transfer the biscuits to a wire rack. The biscuits will continue to crisp up as they cool. Store in an air tight container.

Bake for 2–3 minutes less for a chewier biscuit.

Yoghurt orange and lemon mini cupcakes

These cute cupcakes are manageable mini-mouthfuls for little ones. Adding some yoghurt and citrus fruit keeps them lovely and moist and gives them a deliciously refreshing flavour. They would be great for birthday parties. Suitable for children under 1 year old. Suitable for freezing: un-iced cupcakes can be frozen in a re-sealable box or freezer bag.

Step one Preheat the oven to 180°C/350°F/gas 4 and line a mini-muffin tin with paper cases.

Step two Cream the butter and sugar until pale and fluffy. Gradually add the egg, beating well between additions. Stir in the zests. Sift over the flour and fold in well. Stir in the yoghurt.

Step three Divide the mixture among the mini-muffin cases and bake for 18–20 minutes until risen, lightly golden brown and firm to the touch. Cool in the tins for 5 minutes then transfer to a wire rack and cool completely.

Step four Meanwhile, to make the icing: sift the icing sugar into a bowl. Make a well in the middle and stir in the juices and beat well. Spoon the icing on to the cooled cupcakes and allow to set for up to 30 minutes. Store in an airtight container for up to 5 days.

Makes approx. 18 mini cupcakes

60g (2oz) butter

100g (3½ oz) caster sugar

1 egg, at room temperature

zest of ½ small lemon

zest of ½ lime

½ tsp orange zest

125g (4½ oz) self-raising flour

50ml (2fl oz) natural yoghurt (not low fat)

For the icing

225g (8oz) icing sugar

1 tbsp fresh orange juice

1 tbsp fresh lime juice

Jewelled cupcakes

Let your party girls create their own jewelled cupcakes, topped with a swirl of icing and a variety of 'gems'. You could use ready-made buttercream instead of the cream cheese icing, if you prefer.

Makes 10 cupcakes

125g (4½ oz) butter or margarine

125g (4½ oz) caster sugar

½ tsp lemon zest

2 eggs

125g (4½ oz) self-raising flour

¼ tsp baking powder

Cream cheese icing

110g (4oz) cream cheese, at room temperature

110g (4oz) butter, at room temperature

½ tsp vanilla extract

85g (3oz) icing sugar

edible food colouring

Decorations

edible jewels

jelly beans in bright colours

Jelly Tots

jelly diamonds

Smarties or M&Ms in bright colours

sugar diamonds

Step one Preheat the oven to 180°C/350°F/gas 4 and prepare a 12-hole muffin tin with 10 paper cases.

Step two Cream the butter or margarine in an electric food mixer until soft. Add the sugar and beat until fluffy, then mix in the lemon zest. Add the eggs, one at a time. Add 1 tablespoon of the flour with the second egg, beating continuously. Sift over the remaining flour and baking powder then fold in gently.

Step three Divide the mixture between the paper cases and cook in the oven for about 20 minutes or until golden and springy to the touch. Remove from the oven and cool in the muffin tin for 15 minutes, then transfer to a wire rack to cool completely.

Step four While the cupcakes are baking you can prepare the icing. Beat together the cream cheese and butter. Beat in the vanilla, then sift over the sugar and stir in until the sugar is combined. Beat for 1 minute until fluffy. Transfer to a bowl and set aside in the fridge. If you wish, you can divide the icing into two bowls and colour each with a few drops of different food colourings.

Step five Once the cakes are cold, swirl some of the icing on top of them and stick a selection of decorations into the icing. Leave to stand for around 30 minutes to allow the icing to set.

Party planning: The cakes can be made up to 1 month in advance and frozen, un-iced, in a plastic box. Defrost them at room temperature for around 1 hour, and then ice and decorate as above.

For a video masterclass on icing a cake, go to
www.mykitchentable.co.uk/videos/icing

American-Italian mini
meatballs 162–3
Asian shrimp, sizzling 76–7
bagel snake 150–1
bananas
bread, best ever 10–11
Jamaican muffins 22–3
& peach smoothie 24–5
bars
oat with cranberries, apricots
and pumpkin seeds 20–1
trail mix 168–9
beef
American-Italian mini
meatballs 162–3
Annabel's bolognese 100–1
Annabel's tasty burgers 96–7
diner's blue plate special
meatloaf 92–3
Hungarian goulash 104–5
Nicholas' multi-layered
cottage pie 98–9
& pork meatballs with tagine
sauce 112–13
sesame stir-fry 106–7
stir-fried with noodles 110–11
stroganoff with tagliatelle
90–1
berries
berried treasure 196–7
cherry & berry crush 24–5
cranberry jelly with summer
170–1
frozen with hot white
chocolate sauce 186–7
yoghurt ice, summer 188
bolognese, Annabel's 100–1
bread
best-ever banana 10–11
French toast with caramelised
apples 8–9
Welsh rabbits 12–13
brownies, Lara's favourite
176–7
burgers, Annabel's tasty 96–7
burrito, breakfast 16–17
butternut squash gratin with
penne 122–3
cake

chocolate fridge 178–9
the perfect lemon polenta
174–5
strawberry cream 194–5
cannelloni, chicken 40–1
carrot & apple muffins with
maple syrup 14–15
cheesecake, raspberry ripple
172–3
cherry & berry crush 24–5
chicken
Annabel's pad Thai 26–7
Annabel's paella 62–3
Annabel's pasta salad with
roasted peppers & marinated
52–3
Annabel's rissoles 160–1
basket-weave breasts 42–3
cannelloni 40–1
Caroline's lasagne alfredo
30–1
& corn chowder 142–3
delicious fajitas 36–7
fingers, my favourite 38–9
fruity curry 55–6
Japanese salad 48–9
Karmel 34–5
Little Gem cups 152–3
maple-glazed griddled 32–3
nasi goreng 50–1
satay with Chinese leaf
cabbage, beansprouts &
baby sweetcorn 28–9
soup, Thai-style 56–7
yakitori with noodles 44–5
chocolate
dipped strawberry 'buds'
198, 199
fridge cake 178–9
frozen berries with hot white
sauce 186–7
Lara's favourite brownies
176–7
puddings with fudge sauce
180–1
white chocolate & cranberry
cookies 192–3
chowder, chicken & corn
142–3

coconut shrimp 158–9
cod niçoise, bag-baked 64–5
cookies, cranberry & white
chocolate 192–3
cottage pie, Nicholas'
multi-layered 98–9
cranberries
jelly with summer berries
170–1
& white chocolate cookies
192–3
crisps, baked parsnip & sweet
potato 156–7
crumble, strawberry &
rhubarb 184–5
cupcakes
jewelled 204–5
yoghurt orange & lemon mini
202–3
curry, fruity chicken 55–6
diner's blue special meatloaf
92–3
dip, lemon mayo with krispie
fish fingers 74–5
eggs
bagel snake 150–1
breakfast burrito 16–17
ratatouille omelette 128–9
escalopes with tomatoes &
basil sauce, veal 102–3
fajitas, delicious chicken 36–7
fish pie, mini 80–1
French toast with caramelised
apples 8–9
fridge cake, chocolate 178–9
fruit flowers 198
ginger snaps 200–1
goulash, Hungarian 104–5
Grandma's noodle pudding
166–7
granola, Annabel's 6–7
Gruyère & caramelised onion
tart 126–7
Hungarian goulash 104–5
Jamaican banana muffins 22–3
Japanese chicken salad 48–9
jelly
cranberry with summer
berries 170–1

elderflower 182–3
kebabs, healthy salad 136–7
king prawn curry, mild 78–9
koftas, minty lamb 164–5
lamb
  Annabel's tasty burgers 96–7
  Lloyd's leg of 108–9
  minty koftas 164–5
lasagne
  Caroline's alfredo 30–1
  salmon, prawn & dill 66–7
  spinach, ricotta & tomato 116–17
lemon
  polenta cake, perfect 174–5
  & yoghurt orange mini cupcakes 202–3
Little Gem cups 152–3
lollies
  strawberry sorbet ice 191
  tropical 191
lychee frozen yoghurt, luscious 188
meatballs
  American-Italian mini 162–3
  pork & beef with tagine sauce 112–13
  turkey with spaghetti & tomato sauce 46–7
meatloaf, diner's blue 92–3
minty lamb koftas 164–5
mozzarella & caramelised red onion wraps 146–7
muffins
  apple & carrot with maple syrup 14–15
  Jamaican banana 22–3
nasi goreng 50–1
noodles
  chicken yakitori with 44–5
  pudding, Grandma's 166–7
  sea bass with ginger & spring onion on 88–9
  Singapore 58–9
  stir-fried beef with 110–11
omelette, ratatouille 128–9
onions
  caramelised & Gruyère tart 126–7

  caramelised red & mozzarella wraps 146–7
  soup, Lara's lovely 140–1
orange yoghurt & lemon mini cupcakes 202–3
pad Thai, Annabel's 26–7
paella, Annabel's 62–3
pancakes, Annabel's favourite 18–19
parsnip & sweet potato crisps, baked 156–7
pasta
  Annabel's salad with marinated chicken & roasted peppers 52–3
  bake, spinach & haddock 78–9
  beef stroganoff with tagliatelle 60–1
  butternut squash gratin with penne 122–3
  Caroline's lasagne alfredo 30–1
  chicken cannelloni 40–1
  fusilli with chipolatas & sweet pepper 94–5
  fusilli with salmon & spring vegetables 84–5
  haddock & spinach pasta bake 78–9
  Marina's spaghetti with seafood 72–3
  salad with marinated chicken & roasted peppers 52–3
  salad, turkey 144–5
  salmon, prawn & dill lasagne 66–7
  spaghetti primavera 118–19
  spaghetti with pesto 114–15
  spinach, ricotta & tomato lasagne 116–17
  turkey meatballs with spaghetti & tomato sauce 46–7
  turkey pasta salad 144–5
peach & banana smoothie 24–5
pesto, spaghetti with 114–15
pie

Nicholas' multi-layered cottage pie 98–9
mini fish pie 80–81
tasty salmon & spinach 80–1
pizzas, mini muffin 134–5
pizzette bites, potato 130–1
pork
  American-Italian mini meatballs 162–3
  & beef meatballs with tagine sauce 112–13
prawn
  Annabel's paella 62–3
  coconut shrimp 158–9
  Little Gem cups 152–3
  salmon & dill lasagne 66–7
  sizzling Asian shrimp 76–7
  stir fry with sugar snap peas, king 68–9
  king prawn curry, mild 78–9
rabbits, Welsh 12–13
raspberry ripple cheesecake 172–3
ratatouille omelette 128–9
rhubarb & strawberry crumble 184–5
rice
  Annabel's paella 62–3
  Chinese fried & sticky 82–3
  nasi goreng 50–1
  summer risotto 120–1
  sushi, pressed 71–2
ricotta, spinach & tomato lasagne 116–17
risotto, summer 120–1
salad
  Annabel's pasta with chicken & peppers 52–3
  kebabs, healthy 136–7
  Japanese chicken 48–9
  turkey pasta 144–5
salmon
  fishcakes 86–7
  prawn & dill lasagne 66–7
  sticky & Chinese fried rice 82–3
  teriyaki 60–1
  with fusilli & spring vegetables 84–5

satay, chicken with Chinese
leaf cabbage 28–9
sea bass with ginger & spring
onion on noodles 88–9
shrimp
coconut 158–9
sizzling Asian 76–7
Singapore noodles 58–9
smoothie, peach & banana
24–5
soup
chicken & corn chowder
142–3
Lara's lovely onion 140–1
Thai-style chicken 56–7
tomato 138–9
stir fry
beef with noodles 110–11
king prawn with sugar snap
peas 68–9

sesame beef 106–7
strawberry
chocolate-dipped 'buds' 198,
199
cream cake 194–5
& rhubarb crumble 184–5
sorbet ice lollies 191
sushi, pressed 71–2
sweet potato & parsnip crisps,
baked 156–7
tagliatelle, beef stroganoff
with 90–1
tart, caramelised onion &
Gruyère 126–7
tempura, vegetable 132–3
teriyaki, salmon 60–1
trail mix bars 168–9
tuna
bagel snake 150–1
melt 148–9

turkey
meatballs with spaghetti &
tomato sauce 46–7
pasta salad 144–5
veal
American-Italian mini
meatballs 162–3
escalopes with tomatoes &
basil sauce 102–3
watermelon cooler 191
Welsh rabbits 12–13
wraps
caramelised red onion &
mozzarella 146–7
tasty vegetable 154–5
yakitori, chicken with noodles
44–5
yoghurt
frozen 188–9
ice, summer berry 188

10 9 8 7 6 5 4 3 2

Published in 2011 by Ebury Press, an imprint of Ebury
Publishing

A Random House Group company

Recipes © Annabel Karmel 2011

Book design © Ebury Press 2011

All recipes contained in this book first appeared in *Top
100 Pasta Dishes* (2010), *Top 100 Finger Foods* (2009),
Princess Party Cookbook (2009), *The Fussy Eaters'
Recipe Book* (2007), *After-School Meal Planner* (2006),
Lunchboxes (2003), *Superfoods for Babies and Children*
(2001), *Complete Family Meal Planner* (1999) and
Favourite Family Recipes (1999).

Annable Karmel has asserted her right to be identified as
the author of this Work in accordance with the Copyright,
Designs and Patents Act 1988

The Random House Group Limited

Reg. No. 954009

Addresses for companies within the Random House
Group can be found at www.randomhouse.co.uk

A CIP catalogue record for this book is available from the
British Library

To buy books by your favourite authors and register for
offers visit www.rbooks.co.uk

Printed and bound in the UK by Butler, Tanner and
Dennis Ltd
Colour origination by AltaImage

Commissioning Editor: Muna Reyal
Project Editor: Hannah Knowles
Designer: Lucy Stephens
Photographer: Yuki Sugiura © Ebury Press 2011 (see also
credits below)
Food Stylist: SPK
Props Stylist: Luis Peral
Copy-editor: Michele Clarke
Production: Helen Everson

Photography on page 4 by Muir Vidler © Muir Vidler;
9, 13, 21, 25, 26, 29, 30, 32, 38, 41, 48, 53, 62, 65, 66, 70, 73,
74, 77, 81, 82, 90, 93, 94, 97, 98, 101, 102, 106, 114, 118,
125, 130, 133, 134, 137, 138, 146, 153, 157, 158, 164, 165,
169, 170, 174, 178, 181, 186, 189, 190, 193, 198, 201, 202,
205 © Dave King; 9, 18, 42, 60, 69, 121, 129, 150, 173, 185,
194 © Daniel Pangbourne; 37 © William Lingwood;
9, 14, 45, 85, 143, 154 by Dave King © Annabel Karmel

ISBN: 9780091940539

The Random House Group Limited supports the
Forest Stewardship Council (FSC®), the leading
international forest certification organisation.
Our books carrying the FSC label are printed
on FSC® certified paper. FSC is the only forest
certification scheme endorsed by the leading
environmental organisations, including Greenpeace.
Our paper procurement policy can be found at
www.randomhouse.co.uk/environment